THE
POCKET BOOK
OF
MAN UTD

By Rob Wightman

For Tamsin and Natasha, and in memory of Pat

Published by Vision Sports Publishing in 2010

Vision Sports Publishing
19-23 High Street
Kingston upon Thames
Surrey
KT1 1LL

www.visionsp.co.uk

Text © Rob Wightman
Illustrations © Bob Bond Sporting Caricatures

ISBN: 978-1905326-90-7

Series editor: Jim Drewett
Series production: Martin Cloake
Design: Neal Cobourne
Illustrations: Bob Bond
Cover photography: Paul Downes, Objective Image
All pictures: Getty Images

Printed and bound in China by Toppan Printing Co Ltd

A CIP catalogue record for this book is available from the British Library

THIS IS AN UNOFFICIAL PUBLICATION

All statistics in *The Pocket Book of Man Utd* are correct up until the
end of the 2009/10 season.

CONTENTS

'THE RED DEVILS'

FOREWORD BY
DAVID MAY

When I heard that Manchester United were interested in signing me, I was gobsmacked to be honest. I was happy at Blackburn but, being from Manchester and with a whole family full of Reds, when Fergie came in and gave me the chance to play for the biggest club in the world there was no way I was going to turn it down. I never thought for a minute I'd get a chance like that.

When I went to meet him at the club all we talked about was football. Then he showed me round the museum at Old Trafford. All the old shirts, the trophies, the Busby Babes, Munich, Best, Law and Charlton. The club has moved on to new glories but all that is never forgotten.

That's the thing about United, the history of the club. You can't help feeling part of that when you pull on the famous red shirt. I remember the first time I played for United I was really nervous. Having 55-65,000 people supporting you was just incredible.

The first time I heard my song, "David May, Superstar; He's got more medals than Shearer" I couldn't believe it. I remember at the 1999 FA Cup final against Newcastle our fans were singing it through the whole game. It was amazing. My kids still sing it to me all the time. Even to this day I get stopped and asked about my time at United. It's something I'll never forget, and it's really nice to be remembered.

When I look back on my career at United of course I'm delighted and proud. I just wish I'd won more but I was unlucky with injuries. The highlight for me was winning the Premiership in 1996 at Middlesbrough when I scored the first goal and then playing in the FA Cup final against Liverpool six days later, although everyone remembers the 1999 European Cup final in Barcelona because I managed to get myself into a couple of photos.

I just remember that when the cup was being presented I thought, "get as close as possible to the trophy". I didn't want to be missed out of any of the photos, I wanted to be able to show my children and my grandchildren. I stood up on the stand that the cup had been on and I think Nicky Butt tried to get on it too. It started to buckle but I just held onto the players around me. I might not have played in the match, but it was an historic moment and there I am right in the middle of it.

The great thing about this book is that it sums up all that history. The old pictures and illustrations are wonderful and Rob Wightman has done a great job in capturing what Manchester United is all about. I hope you enjoy it as much as I did.

...CLUB DIRECTORY...

Club address: Manchester United
Sir Matt Busby Way, Old Trafford
Manchester, M16 0RA

Supporters General Enquiries Line:
+44 (0) 161 868 8000

Ticket Sales and Match Information Line:
+44 (0) 161 868 8000;
tickets@manutd.co.uk

One United Membership: +44 (0) 161 868 8000;
membership@manutd.co.uk

Hospitality: +44 (0) 161 868 8000;
commercial@manutd.co.uk

Disabled Supporters Association (MUDSA):
+44 (0) 845 230 1989;
disability@manutd.co.uk

Text Phone for Deaf/Impaired
Hearing: +44 (0) 161 868 8668
Programme and Magazine
Subscriptions:
+44 (0) 845 677 7801;
www.manutd.com/programme

Megastore:

+44 (0) 161 868 8567;

megastore@manutd.co.uk

Mail Order: UK:

0870 111 8107;

Overseas:

+44 (0) 115 907 1852

Museum and Tour Enquiries:

+44 (0) 161 868 8000;

tours@manutd.co.uk

Red Café (Old Trafford):

+44 (0) 161 868 8000

MUTV Subscriptions: 0870 848 6888

MUTV Enquiries: 0161 834 1111

MU Travel: 0870 112 0274

Manchester United Foundation:

0161 868 8600;

enquiries@mufoundation.org

Football in the Community:

0161 708 9451;

football@mufoundation.org

Club website: www.manutd.com

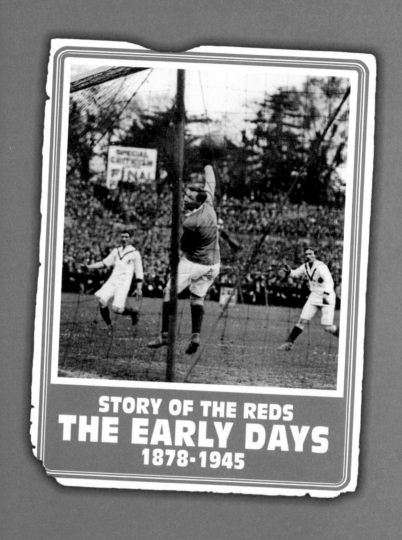

STORY OF THE REDS
THE EARLY DAYS
1878-1945

United's status as one of the world's elite football clubs, with a fan base that stretches from Salford to Stockholm and Trafford Park to Tokyo, could hardly be further removed from its modest late 19th century roots.

The club's first players and supporters were the men of the Carriage and Wagon department of the Lancashire and Yorkshire Railway who, in 1878, formed Newton Heath LYR. The first home games, against other sections of the LYR and other railway companies, were played at North Road near the Newton Heath railway yard. The players changed into their distinctive green and gold shirts in local pubs.

Newton Heath FC in 1892, the year the club joined the Football League

Newton Heath collected their first trophy, the Manchester Cup, in 1886 but their application to join the Football League, when it was created two years

later, was rejected. Wanting progress, the club left North Road for Bank Street in the district of Clayton.

When the Heathens finally gained entry to Division One of the Football League, they struggled. They lost their first match at Blackburn Rovers on 3rd September 1892, and did not win until the 10-1 thrashing of Wolverhampton Wanderers six weeks later. They finished bottom, and only saved their top-flight status by beating Small Heath, soon to become Birmingham City, in a play-off. But defeat to Liverpool in the next season's play-off consigned them to 12 seasons in the second tier.

Brewer John Henry Davies renamed the club Manchester United

By February 1901, a severe financial crisis threatened the club's existence. To raise funds, a bazaar was held at St James's Hall. The resourceful captain, Harry Stafford, brought along his St. Bernard dog, with a collection box fastened around its neck. But the dog wandered off and was found by an affluent local brewer, John Henry Davies, who was so intrigued that he contributed to the club's appeal. When Newton Heath were declared bankrupt a year later, Davies and his associates paid off most of the £2,670 debt in return for control.

Davies's first act on becoming club president was to insist on a name change. "Manchester Central" and "Manchester Celtic" were proposed, but "Manchester United", suggested by Louis Rocca, a long-serving

In 1907/08, the club won the first of many League Championships

club official, had the most resonance. The club's colours would now be red and white, while new offices were established at the Imperial Hotel.

The revolution continued with the appointment of Ernest Mangnall from Burnley as secretary-manager. Mangnall was, the *Manchester Evening News* reported, "a gentleman well versed in football matters".

He recruited steely performers such as centre half
Charlie Roberts and half backs Alex Bell and Dick
Duckworth and, in Mangnall's third season, United
gained promotion and reached the quarter-finals of
the FA Cup.

At that time, Manchester City were regarded as

Billy Meredith in action against QPR in 1908, during the first ever FA Charity Shield

Manchester's premier team, since they had won the FA Cup and established themselves in the top flight. But City were in trouble after an FA inquiry into allegations of financial irregularities resulted in 17 players receiving lifetime bans.

Mangnall took advantage, signing City forwards Sandy Turnbull and Jimmy Bannister, plus full back Herbert Burgess. But the biggest prize was winger Billy Meredith, dubbed the Welsh Wizard for his pace and trickery.

In 1907/08, United romped to their first-ever League title, with a record 52 points from 38 games – it was two points for a win back then. More silverware followed in 1908/09 when they defeated Queens Park Rangers in the inaugural Charity Shield, then

The 1909 FA Cup
winners show off
the trophy

lifted their first FA Cup. Bristol City were beaten in the Crystal Palace final, thanks to Turnbull's only goal of the game. Huge crowds lined the streets of Manchester to greet the returning heroes.

But in the close season a row broke out when the Football League suspended a group of players, led by Meredith, because they were members of the banned Players' Union. The group responded by forming a breakaway team, "The Outcasts FC", until, on the eve of the new season, the League relented and recognised the union.

In February 1910, United moved to a new 100,000 capacity stadium. Life at Old Trafford started with defeat to Liverpool, but United soon turned their new home into a fortress and, in 1911, they again won the title – their last for over four decades.

Despite the 8–4 thrashing of Swindon Town in the Charity Shield, United finished a disappointing 13th the next season, after which Mangnall decamped to Manchester City.

Having delivered two League titles, the FA Cup and two Charity Shields, he was a hard act to follow. Stalwarts like Bell and Roberts were sold and crowds dwindled. In December 1915, with Britain now at war, news broke of a match-fixing scandal. Following an inquiry, United's Enoch West, Arthur Whalley and

The Red Army arrive at Euston station for a cup tie against Arsenal in 1937

Sandy Turnbull were banned for life, as were four Liverpool players and one Chester player. Turnbull, the forward who was integral to United's success under Mangnall, went to fight in France, where he was killed in May 1917.

United's downward spiral continued after the war. They were relegated in 1922, a year after fans' favourite Meredith returned to City. For the next 17 seasons, United yo-yoed between the first and second divisions. None of the six managers employed between 1912 and the outbreak of the second war could bring stability. Attendances fell and the club felt the pinch, especially after the death in October 1927 of JH Davies, its president and principal benefactor.

United reached the brink of extinction four years later, when manager Walter Crickmer was told by the bank that there would be no more credit. Who now would bankroll a club whose fans were boycotting matches in protest at the team's relegation in 1931 and the way the club was run?

Enter James Gibson, a charismatic textile magnate, who took over as president having pledged a £30,000 rescue package. By 1939, Britain was at war again and the league was suspended, but Gibson had brought stability and United had cemented their status as a Division One side after 1938's promotion.

Youth development, Gibson believed, was the key to future success, so he established the Manchester United Junior Athletic Club to identify and nurture young talent. When the war ended, he just needed to find a manager who shared his vision.

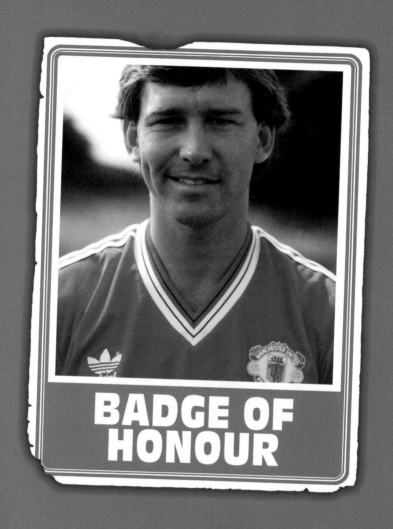

BADGE OF
HONOUR

As you might expect with a club that has changed its home ground more than once and even changed its name, Manchester United's badge has undergone several alterations over the years.

What is perhaps surprising, especially for fans living in an era when even pub teams have carefully designed logos, is that the badge didn't appear on the club shirt until as late as the 1972/73 season.

The only exception was when United played in a cup final. Then, a special shirt would be made. When Ernest Mangnall's team became the first United side to reach – and win – an FA Cup final in 1909, the red rose of Lancashire was added to their shirts.

Shirts for the FA Cup finals of 1948, 1957 and 1963 and the 1968 European Cup final bore a badge based on the coat of arms of the city of Manchester. The early versions of this crest feature an antelope and a lion supporting a shield decorated with red and brown stripes and a sailing ship. The ship, travelling across an expanse of water, represents the city's tradition of commercial enterprise and its

Special shirts with badges were worn for Cup Finals, here in 1948

links to the sea. Above the shield is a globe with bees buzzing around it, symbolising Manchester's trade links across the world.

Below the shield a motto reads Concilio et Labore, which is Latin for "Wisdom and Endeavour". Such qualities came in handy for Matt Busby's United sides, who lost only once while wearing this badge – in the 1957 FA Cup final to Aston Villa. The motto still appears on the official club blazers that players and staff wear for formal occasions, including cup finals.

However, a different badge appeared on the shirts United wore for the 1958 FA Cup final, which they lost to Bolton Wanderers just three months after the Munich tragedy. By coincidence, the Manchester coat of arms was redesigned that year to include an armoured helmet and red mantling on which eagles fly. A similar eagle

From the 1940s, the club crest reflected the city's commercial and trading status

A new badge appeared on the 1958 FA Cup final shirts

formed the centrepiece of United's badge for the final. The bird sat on a crown with "Wembley" above and "1958" below. A large "M" was superimposed on the bird's breast.

During the halcyon days of the 1960s, the club developed its own badge. Circular in design, the top semi-circle read "Manchester United" and the bottom read "Football Club". A football on either side separated the two semi-circles, which were both adorned with curly golden labels. The Manchester shield and ship remained in the central part.

The 'Wisdom and endeavour' motto and crest still adorn the club's official blazers

This badge was used in the club's programme, *United Review*, in the 1960s. Around the same time, club merchandise started using an image of a red devil, inspired by the club's nickname which also emerged in the 1960s. The red devil replaced the three stripes on the shield in the centre of the

From the 1960s onwards, the club began to develop its own badge

22

badge when it first appeared on the United shirt worn by the likes of Bobby Charlton and George Best in the 1972/73 season.

By the mid-1970s, it also appeared on the players' shorts. There was a minor change to the badge when United celebrated their centenary in 1978/79. For that season only it included the dates 1878 and 1978, with "Manchester United Football Club" replaced by "Manchester United Centenary". Unfortunately, the change could not prevent Dave Sexton's team losing 3-2 to Arsenal in the 1979 FA Cup final.

During the 1980s, when Adidas supplied the club's kit, the curly labels on the badge were replaced by Adidas boots. In 1998, as part of a re-branding programme, the words "Football Club" were removed and the ship, hitherto yellow on a white background, was changed to yellow on red. While many would argue that a football club's badge should somewhere bear the words "Football Club", their removal brought good luck: United won the 1999 Treble soon after the change.

The club's current badge, with the words 'Football Club' nowhere to be seen

Between 1997 and 2000, the badge used on the club's special European kit was placed on a background of a white triangular shield. Wearing this badge United overcame Bayern Munich at Camp Nou, Barcelona, to win the 1999 European Cup.

"YOU'LL WIN NOTHING WITH KIDS"

Matt Busby recognised that Manchester United could become a major force by finding and nurturing its own talent. This approach would allow Busby to mould players from an early age so that they espoused the new club ethos of total commitment and attractive attacking football. And players who had grown up together would enjoy exceptional camaraderie, always a benefit in team sports.

The manager set up an extensive scouting network in northern England, Wales, Scotland and all Ireland, establishing a logical system of progression whereby players would move up to more senior sides as they matured, culminating in a first-team career for the most talented. Youngsters offered a place in the United youth system were billeted with a landlady or local family who would provide a supportive and homely environment.

Overall responsibility for youth development was placed in the capable hands of Busby's assistant, Jimmy Murphy. When the system finally bore fruit, the results were spectacular. United won the FA Youth Cup five seasons running after its inception in 1953. That same year Duncan Edwards, arguably United's greatest-ever home-grown talent, made his first-team debut. More youngsters flooded into the senior ranks, Busby knowing precisely when each was ready, and his side was soon dubbed the Busby Babes. Of the 1956 and 1957 title-winning sides, eight regulars were homegrown. Sadly, many, including Edwards, were lost in the Munich air crash.

Eight of the 1957 FA Cup-winning team were homegrown

The youth system was the foundation on which Busby built his next great side. Eight of the team that defeated Benfica in the European Cup final a decade after Munich had come the youth route. They included Bobby Charlton, George Best and Nobby Stiles – true legends of the game.

Fast forward to November 1986. When Alex Ferguson succeeded Ron Atkinson he was "appalled by the shortcomings of our scouting network". Yet the new boss was determined to create "a youth policy that would be the envy of every club in Britain". Ferguson instructed his scouts to innovate. Emphasis should be placed on quality, not quantity. The process required patience. It was almost five years before a top-drawer player emerged. Happily, however, Ryan Giggs was worth the wait.

While Giggs was establishing himself in the first team, a side featuring David Beckham, Nicky Butt and Gary Neville was winning the 1992 FA Youth Cup. Over the next few seasons these three, plus Paul Scholes and Phil Neville, were gradually introduced to the senior side. After the departure of several big names in the summer of 1995, Ferguson opted to promote internally. But when United lost 3-1 at Aston Villa on the opening day of 1995/96, some suggested that the capability of Fergie's Fledglings had been overestimated. "You'll never win anything with kids," spouted *Match of the Day* pundit Alan Hansen.

Nine months later United celebrated a League and Cup double in which Giggs, Beckham, the Nevilles, Butt and Scholes had played a full part. Such success prompted a memorable retort to Hansen from Eric Harrison, who coached the Beckham generation at youth level. "Win nothing with kids? Depends on the kids, doesn't it?"

Just three years later these "kids" helped United land an unprecedented treble of the Premier League, FA Cup and Champions League. In the ensuing years, Wes Brown, Darren Fletcher and John O'Shea graduated from the reserves. Many such players have been blooded in cup competitions, especially the League Cup, which Ferguson uses smartly for youth development.

As United have thrived, the demands on the squad have increased – especially in 2008/09 when they played almost 70 games across five competitions. Again, products of the youth system helped deliver trophies. Centre half Jonny Evans proved his ability in all competitions, Danny Welbeck and Darron Gibson featured in the League Cup triumph, and Italian striker Federico Macheda scored two crucial winners to sustain the title charge.

Macheda is not strictly homegrown – he was lured from Lazio at 16 after United exploited Italian regulations which prevent under-18s from signing professional. Premier League restrictions on the recruitment of English youngsters – 12 to 16-year-olds must live within 90 minutes of Old Trafford to be eligible for the United Academy – have encouraged talent-spotting further afield. Brazilian twins Fabio and Rafael Da Silva, snapped up from Fluminense, also contributed to the success of 2008/09 and beyond.

Former players who are part of the youth setup include academy director Brian McClair and reserves manager Ole Gunnar Solskjaer. The academy takes boys from under-nine to under-18 level. Its senior team plays in the Academy League in north west and central England. Those who graduate join the reserves and play in the Premier Reserve League against teams from northern England.

Emphasis is always on the development of technique and intelligent movement, which is why many of the younger age groups play innovative four-against-four games. "We want young players who were brought up at this club the right way, and to understand what playing for this football club is," Ferguson said. "And the younger you get them, the better it is."

David Beckham is probably the biggest star the youth system has produced

OLD TRAFFORD

For all the classic matches it has hosted and the gifted players who have graced its turf, Old Trafford is not United's original home. As Newton Heath, the club played at North Road from 1878 until moving to Bank Street in Clayton in 1893. Almost a decade later, J H Davies rescued the club from bankruptcy and renamed it Manchester United. Wanting a ground that could hold far more than Bank Street's 50,000 capacity, Davies invested £60,000 in a plot in Old Trafford, about two miles south west of Manchester city centre.

Old Trafford opened officially on 19th February 1910, when around 50,000 spectators saw United lose narrowly to Liverpool. The ground had excellent transport links, a capacity of 80,000, and modern facilities including a gymnasium. The players took to Old Trafford, clinching the League title within 18 months of moving home. Soon it hosted FA Cup semi-finals, and even the 1915 final between Sheffield United and Chelsea.

While the team fell into a lengthy decline after the 1911 title triumph, Old Trafford enhanced its reputation as a leading venue. The ground's attendance record was established in March 1939, when 79,962 people squeezed in for the FA Cup semi-final between Wolves and Grimsby. But during the Second World War it was hit by German bombs targeting the nearby

industrial estate. The Main Stand was almost
demolished, the United Road terrace damaged, and
the pitch scorched.

Homeless when the Football League resumed
after the war, United paid Manchester City £5,000
a season to use Maine Road for their home games
while Old Trafford was reconstructed. The rebuilding
lasted four years and cost around £25,000. United
finally returned home in August 1949, beating Bolton

Old Trafford in 1930,
amidst the houses and
factories of Manchester

3-0, but Old Trafford's full capacity was not restored for five more years.

Over the next decade, floodlights were added, the Stretford End was covered, seats were added to the United Road side of the stadium, and cantilever stands were developed on the north and east sides. Old Trafford staged group games for the 1966 World Cup finals – an apt reward for the ongoing development chairman Louis Edwards and manager Matt Busby had first envisaged in the early 1960s

The Stretford End in full voice in 1980

Further improvements increased capacity to over
60,000 for much of the 1970s. Important additions
included 10,000 seats in the United Road Stand and
5,500 seats at the Scoreboard End. This area, called K
Stand, soon earned a reputation for its vocal support.
By 1985, the cantilever roof covered three quarters
of the stands. But the planned new Stretford End
featured both a standing paddock and seating, which
meant it could not be built once the Taylor Report
into the Hillsborough disaster of 1989 recommended

OLD TRAFFORD

BUILT: 1949
LOCATION: OLD TRAFFORD, MANCHESTER
CAPACITY: 76,212

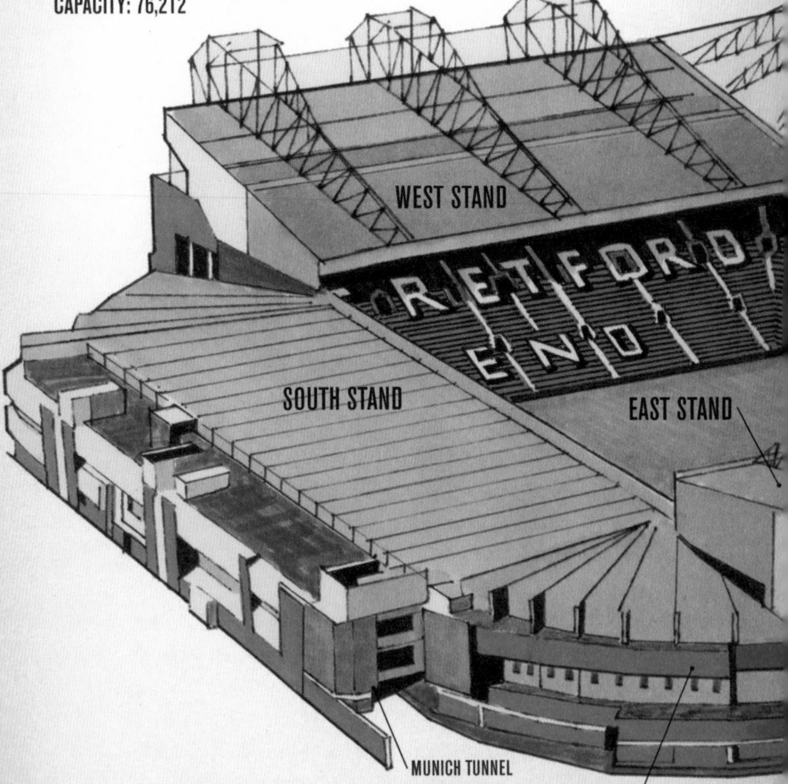

WEST STAND

RETFORD END

SOUTH STAND

EAST STAND

MUNICH TUNNEL
AND PLAYERS'
ENTRANCE

MUNICH CLOCK

MUNI
MEMORI
PLAQ

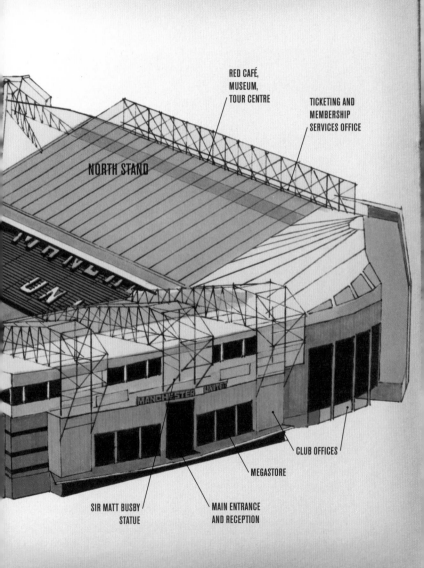

RED CAFÉ, MUSEUM, TOUR CENTRE

TICKETING AND MEMBERSHIP SERVICES OFFICE

NORTH STAND

MANCHESTER UNITED

CLUB OFFICES

MEGASTORE

SIR MATT BUSBY STATUE

MAIN ENTRANCE AND RECEPTION

IN MEMORY OF THE OFFICIALS & PLAYERS WHO LOST THEIR LIVES

WALTER CRICKMER   TOM CURRY

BERT W'HALLEY

ROGER BYRNE

GEOFF BENT   MARK JONES
EDDIE COLMAN   DAVID PEGG
DUNCAN EDWARDS   TOMMY TAYLOR
BILLY   WHELAN

IN THE MUNICH AIR DISASTER ON THE 6TH FEBRUARY 1958

that all top-flight stadiums be converted to all-seaters. To comply with the new requirements, the club spent £10 million transforming the Stretford End into a stand to seat 10,164 spectators.

A memorial to the Munich victims is built into the fabric of the modern stadium

The all-seating requirement cut Old Trafford's capacity to just under 45,000 at a time when the successful, exciting teams of the 1990s were creating great demand for tickets. The club responded by constructing a vast new stand on the United Road side, at a cost of almost £19 million. The North Stand seats 25,300 people in its three tiers. It was completed in time for the ground, whose capacity was now 55,000, to host group games, a quarter-final and a semi-final of Euro 96.

Still demand for tickets exceeded supply, and soon after United collected the Treble in May 1999 another expansion programme began. Over three years a further 6,200 seats were added to both the East and West stands, increasing capacity to 67,400. The most recent expansions have pushed capacity up to 76,212. United's defeat of Blackburn Rovers on 31st March 2007 was attended by 76,098 spectators, a Premier League record and Old Trafford's highest attendance as an all-seater.

The four stands are now named, rather unimaginatively, according to their geographical position. The North Stand was originally called the United Road Stand. The South Stand was previously Old Trafford's main stand. The East Stand was the Scoreboard End, for obvious reasons.

The West Stand is still better known as the Stretford End, famous as the part of the ground that offered the loudest encouragement to the team. Which is partly why many fans from K Stand chose to relocate here when the second tier was built in 2000. This end is adorned with banners celebrating great moments and figures in United history.

The dugouts sit at the bottom of the South Stand, either side of the old tunnel, renamed the Munich Tunnel in 2008. The tunnel from which the players now emerge is located in the south west corner of the ground. For many match-goers, the downside of the modern Old Trafford is the lack of noise generated by the huge crowds – a sentiment echoed by Sir Alex Ferguson. Some blame the large numbers of tourist supporters and suits on corporate jollies for diluting the atmosphere.

Other than United games, Old Trafford has hosted England internationals, European finals and FA Cup semi-finals, as well as rugby league finals, rugby union internationals, and concerts by artists like Bruce Springsteen and Simply Red. Facilities at the stadium include a splendid museum, plush hospitality suites, the Megastore, the Red Café, and modern club offices behind the glass facade of the East Stand.

The Munich Clock and a plaque remember those who perished in 1958. A life-size bronze statue of Sir Matt Busby honours the great man. And a statue of Best, Charlton and Law celebrates the contribution of the so-called United Trinity and the club's first-ever European Cup. For all the changes, Old Trafford has not lost touch with its heritage.

The modern Old Trafford, styled The Theatre of Dreams

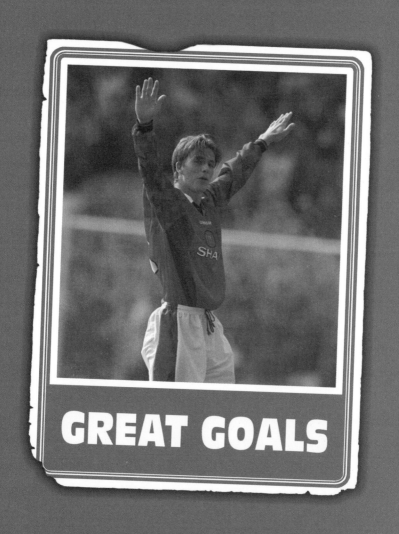

GREAT GOALS

NORMAN WHITESIDE
1983 FA CUP SEMI-FINAL V ARSENAL

Not for the last time, a spectacular intervention by a United player saw off Arsenal in a thrilling semi-final at Villa Park.

This match was how cup football used to be: a helter-skelter, end-to-end affair in which no prisoners were taken. Arsenal went ahead through Tony Woodcock, but Ron Atkinson's United responded after the interval when skipper Bryan Robson fired home the equaliser past George Wood. The pace and intensity of the match then increased as both sides searched for a winner.

With 20 minutes remaining, Arsenal's Vladimir Petrovic hooked a long clearance towards the halfway line, where Gordon McQueen nipped ahead of Woodcock to win possession. The centre half chested the ball carefully to Arthur Albiston, who was stationed on the left flank.

The full back also controlled it on his chest before launching a speculative high ball into the Arsenal box, and while the Gunners' backline looked for a non-existent offside, Whiteside raced into the inside-left channel.

As the ball bounced up invitingly, the 17-year-old Irish striker set himself before unleashing a fierce left-foot volley beyond Wood and into the far corner of the Arsenal net. "Absolutely perfect!" raved John Motson in the *Match of the Day* commentary box.

Whiteside was on the scoresheet again as United thrashed Brighton 4-0 in the FA Cup final replay.

ERIC CANTONA
1996 PREMIER LEAGUE V SUNDERLAND

Even in a season when his form fluctuated and his goal-scoring touch sometimes deserted him, Cantona produced a moment of magic that few could emulate.

With United already 4-0 up in the second half, David May slid a pass from right back, over the halfway line, to the Frenchman, who received the ball with his back to goal.

Cantona pirouetted, outfoxing the two Sunderland players who converged on him, and strode menacingly into opposition territory.

When the next defender came to challenge, Cantona flicked the ball inside to Brian McClair, who eased it straight back into the Frenchman's path as he ran into the Sunderland penalty area.

Cantona looked up, saw that Lionel Perez had come off his line, and chipped the ball delicately over the goalkeeper, onto the inside of the far post and into the top corner of the net.

The United captain celebrated his first league goal from open play for over three months by raising his arms slowly and turning to milk the applause that reverberated around Old Trafford.

"What remains most vividly in my mind is Eric's response," Alex Ferguson remembered. "It was the look of him, as if he was saying: 'Don't ever doubt me. I know I haven't been playing as well as I can, but I'm back and here's to the memories.'"

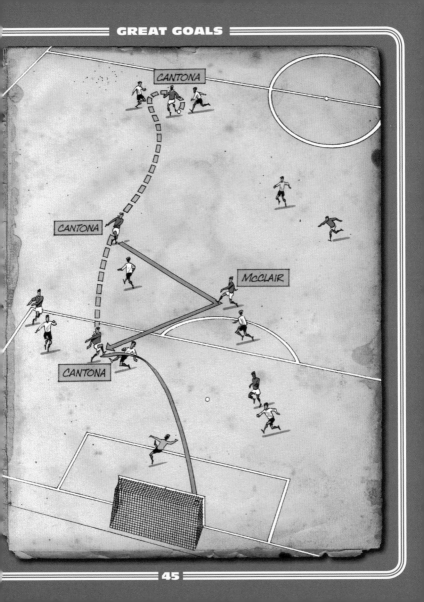

CANTONA

CANTONA

McCLAIR

CANTONA

DAVID BECKHAM
1996 PREMIER LEAGUE V WIMBLEDON

It took only one majestic strike of his right boot to transform David Beckham from being an impressive youngster to a superstar who would attract incessant attention across the globe.

Goals from Eric Cantona and Denis Irwin meant United were cruising to victory when Ronny Johnsen seized possession midway inside his own half. The midfielder quickly laid the ball off to Brian McClair, who flicked it on to Beckham.

The 21-year-old allowed the ball to run forward as he assessed his options. There was little on. Ahead of him, infield, striker Jordi Cruyff was in space, but would soon be outnumbered by Wimbledon defenders.

Moments earlier Cruyff had made an audacious long-range attempt to chip Dons goalkeeper Neil Sullivan – and perhaps that's what gave Beckham the idea.

As the ball rolled onto the halfway line, to the right of the centre circle, the young midfielder, having spotted that Sullivan was off his line, struck a perfectly-weighted shot that looped over the stranded goalkeeper.

"I thought it would be close because I'd hit it perfectly," Beckham recalled. "On the bench, Alex Ferguson said he was muttering: 'Oh, trust him.' A couple of seconds later, I was celebrating one of the most incredible moments of my career."

Even Cantona was impressed by the man who would inherit his number seven shirt, and said: "Beautiful goal, David."

BECKHAM

McCLAIR

BECKHAM

CRUYFF

ANDY COLE
1998 CHAMPIONS LEAGUE GROUP STAGE V BARCELONA

It was fitting that United played some of their most breathtaking football of the Treble season on the ground where they had been humiliated four years earlier by the Barcelona Dream Team.

With 53 minutes of a pulsating encounter gone and the score at 1-1, Paul Scholes slid a square pass to Roy Keane on the United right. Keane advanced into Barcelona territory before pushing the ball inside towards Dwight Yorke.

Yorke feinted, as if to collect the ball, but let it run to his strike partner Andy Cole in a central position ten yards from the edge of the Barcelona penalty area. The pair were on the same wavelength and Cole returned the ball first time to Yorke, who was now rushing towards the box.

Without controlling the ball, Yorke played it straight back into Cole's path. Barça's defence was split by such clever and rapid interplay, and Cole fired home past the advancing Ruud Hesp for a goal of pure genius.

Though the match ended in a 3-3 draw, the Reds now had the self-belief to perform away from home on the biggest stage. And the partnership between Cole and Yorke, who struck twice that night, was creating shockwaves all across Europe.

The next time they visited Camp Nou, they were crowned European champions.

KEANE

SCHOLES

KEANE

YORKE

YORKE

COLE

COLE

RYAN GIGGS
1999 FA CUP SEMI-FINAL REPLAY V ARSENAL

The words "rather weary one from Vieira", uttered by Sky commentator Martin Tyler, entered into United folklore for what happened next.

At the moment when the Arsenal midfielder's sloppy cross-field pass was collected by Ryan Giggs, a penalty shootout represented the best hope of reaching Wembley for United, who were down to ten men after the dismissal of Roy Keane.

But Giggs was fresher than most, having been introduced as a substitute after an hour of an encounter that was now entering its 109th minute. The winger showed his sprightliness as he raced over halfway and avoided the challenge of the retreating Vieira. Then he slalomed between Lee Dixon and Martin Keown on the edge of the Arsenal box, while Dwight Yorke made a decoy run to his left.

As Giggs charged into the inside-left channel, Tony Adams slid in with a last-ditch challenge that could not prevent the Welshman from hammering the ball into the roof of David Seaman's net.

Giggs wheeled away in celebration, removing his shirt and twirling it around above his head. Not even the sight of his hairy chest could discourage United's players and fans from mobbing their hero.

"That has to be one of the best goals ever scored in major football," Alex Ferguson reflected on the strike that gave United a 2-1 victory and booked their place in the final.

GIGGS

YORKE

GIGGS

PAUL SCHOLES
2003 PREMIER LEAGUE V NEWCASTLE

"I was expecting to see a few goals, but I hardly thought it would end up being a 6-2 thriller," said Sir Alex Ferguson after seeing his side obliterate Newcastle at St James' Park and climb to the top of the table for the first time that season.

Given licence to roam by the presence of Roy Keane and Nicky Butt in central midfield, Scholes was instrumental in a United away display that was as devastating as any in Premier League history.

Eleven minutes before the break, with the score at 1-1, left back John O'Shea collected the ball midway inside the Newcastle half. He slid a pass forward to Scholes, who evaded the challenge of Titus Bramble and squared the ball to Ole Gunnar Solskjaer, the scorer of United's first goal.

The Norwegian looped a return pass to Scholes as the diminutive midfielder burst into the inside left position. Almost without breaking stride, Scholes smashed a powerful volley past Shay Given's right hand to put the visitors ahead.

Scholes later completed a hat-trick, and there were also goals from Ryan Giggs and Ruud van Nistelrooy in a win that set United on the road to their fourth title in five years.

"It was awesome," enthused Ferguson. "Newcastle scored first but that only seemed to urge us into more impressive form, with Paul Scholes man of the match."

SCHOLES

SCHOLES

SOLSKJAER

O'SHEA

CRISTIANO RONALDO

2008 CHAMPIONS LEAGUE QUARTER-FINAL V ROMA

One great leap by Ronaldo, one giant leap for United on a marvellous night at the Stadio Olimpico.

The Portuguese finally proved his ability to be a matchwinner on the big occasion, while the Reds recovered from the travel sickness that had blighted their every attempt to conquer Europe since 1999.

It was a tense occasion and chances were scarce until Ronaldo intervened six minutes before the break. The move began with John O'Shea, who had just come on for the injured Nemanja Vidic, slipping a pass forward to Wayne Rooney.

The striker shielded the ball before losing his marker with a clever turn and advancing to the edge of the penalty area, where his pass released Paul Scholes on the United right.

When Scholes clipped a cross above the penalty spot, Roma had plenty of men back. But nobody picked up the late, lung-busting run of Ronaldo, who had sprinted 50 yards. He launched himself at the ball and scored with a towering header.

It was the breakthrough United craved, and Rooney later added a second to make their semi-final place almost certain. "Ronaldo's goal changed the game for us," purred Sir Alex Ferguson. "It was a centre forward's header – it reminded me of myself."

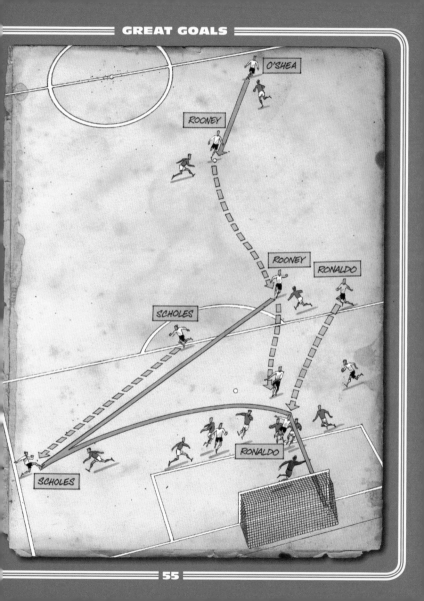

O'SHEA

ROONEY

ROONEY

RONALDO

SCHOLES

SCHOLES

RONALDO

FROM THE CLIFF TO CARRINGTON

Just as musicians toil for hours in rehearsal rooms perfecting their sound before playing live, a football team grafts at the training ground in preparation for match day. The training ground is where the players build fitness, hone skills, practise set-plays and receive treatment for injuries. Where new signings and young bucks are integrated into the senior squad. Where the manager gives tactical instructions and experiments with variations in system and formation. Where he explains to individuals any special role he has for them, or offers personal encouragement, or even rebukes them for breaches of discipline. All this has one aim: to create a winning team.

In early 2000, United's training base moved from The Cliff to the ultramodern Trafford Training Centre. In doing so, they left behind half a century of memories. Generations of talented youngsters, from Duncan Edwards to Paul Scholes, were nurtured to stardom at The Cliff. The Busby Babes had their last training session there before

George Best enjoys a relaxing bath after training at The Cliff…

the fateful trip to Belgrade in February 1958.

Team-mates Remi Moses and Jesper Olsen infamously came to blows there during a five-a-side match in the Ron Atkinson era. A 13-year-old Ryan Giggs made a lasting impression on Alex Ferguson with a trial at The Cliff that the manager described as "one of those rare and priceless moments". And Eric Cantona surprised his new boss and team-mates by doing extra practice after his first training session there.

... and waits for treatment on the physio's table at the same venue in 1965

United bought The Cliff, situated in the Broughton area of Greater Manchester, in 1951 from the Broughton Rangers rugby league club. Training had hitherto taken place at Old Trafford, but Matt Busby was concerned about the damage this was doing to the pitch, especially since he was striving to engender a style of play based on passing and movement. Such a facility was also central to Busby's plans to build a youth system that would provide the personnel for the first team in the long term.

Under Busby, there was a practice match on Tuesdays. On the other mornings, the players would do running for fitness, plus some sprints and a bit of gym work. Sometimes, as Wilf McGuinness put it, they went "straight round the back for the game". McGuinness added: "We used to play on the car park, which was half cinders, half tar." Hardly the sort of surface one can envisage David

Beckham or Cristiano Ronaldo using for practice.

While Busby's players were going through their paces one morning in 1961, the manager was informed that he was to be made a freeman of the city of Manchester. "Don't let the boys know yet," he quipped to reporters at The Cliff. "They'll stop training."

Like all English training grounds, United's is used every day of the year. "I couldn't believe how many autograph hunters were there at The Cliff today. It's Christmas Day, for Christsakes!" Phil Neville revealed in his diary for the 1997/98 season. But despite The Cliff's cherished status among players and supporters, the club decided that the new millennium required a state-of-the-art training complex.

Located on a 108-acre site in Carrington, Greater Manchester, the Trafford Training Centre boasts a mind-boggling array of facilities. Known simply as Carrington, it has 12 grass pitches, including one with undersoil heating for use by the first team. Other amenities include a training rehab pool, weights room, swimming pool, hydrotherapy pool, spa pool, sauna, changing rooms, laundry room, kit and boot rooms, physio treatment room, doctor's room, classroom, kitchens and the players' canteen, plus, of course, Sir Alex Ferguson's office.

The February 2005 issue of the club's official magazine revealed that there were 1,300 lights at Carrington – much to the dismay of environmentalists, one imagines. At least the astro-turf pitches are made partly from recycled car tyres.

Carrington provides facilities for all United's teams, from the senior side right down to the Academy under-nines.

But the move there did not entail a complete break with the past since The Cliff hosts many of United's Football in the Community projects, including sessions for disabled players and holiday courses for schoolchildren.

Carrington has been dubbed "Fortress Carrington" and "Fort Knox" because of the 2.4 km of fencing that surrounds it, the tight security and lack of public access. The club doesn't want spies from other teams or journalists to know its training methods and plans for specific matches. Even more understandably, United, like most clubs, see the need to protect multi-million-pound assets from modern ills like terrorist attacks.

Approved members of the press are restricted to certain areas away from the training pitches, although there are occasional press days when sessions are opened up to journalists and photographers. Many fans and journalists long for the days when they could just turn up at The Cliff and watch the players in training. Understandably so since the experience of witnessing at such close quarters players like George Best, Bobby Charlton, Bryan Robson or Cantona must have been truly special. The end of that era, it seems, is the price of progress.

Wayne Rooney and his team-mates enjoy the benefits of a state-of-the-art training ground at Carrington

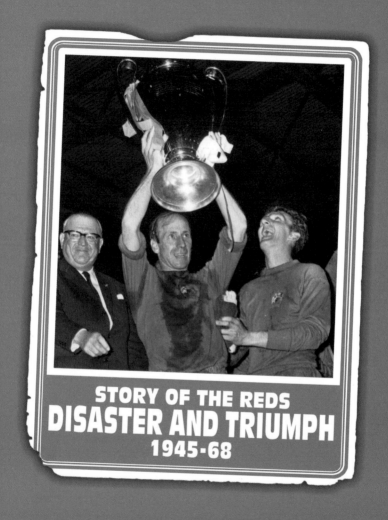

STORY OF THE REDS
DISASTER AND TRIUMPH
1945-68

As the war ended in 1945, Matt Busby approached United to propose himself as the club's next manager. A former Liverpool and Manchester City player, Busby had coached a wartime British Army touring team that included Stanley Matthews.

James Gibson saw that Busby shared his drive to build a successful club based on homegrown talent and agreed to a five-year contract that gave Busby wide-ranging powers. "He [Busby] will build up the team and put it right where it belongs – at the top," Walter Crickmer, the United secretary, told the *Manchester Evening News*.

When Busby took charge in October 1945, he appointed Jimmy Murphy, a former Welsh international, as his assistant to oversee youth development. Busby, now 36, overhauled the squad before the Football League, suspended during the war, resumed in August 1946. Several players were sold, Johnny Carey was switched from inside forward to full back, where he prospered, and Busby recruited new blood, including forward Jimmy Delaney from Celtic.

The crowds that packed into Maine Road – Old Trafford was being rebuilt after the blitz – craved entertainment as escapism from the horrors of the war. They were not disappointed: United won their first five matches, including the 5-0 hammering of Liverpool in September 1946. "We played one touch, or just two touches, no more," half back Henry

Cockburn recalled. "It was flowing all the time."

The reward for this attacking approach was United's first-ever trip to Wembley, in April 1948. Twice they fell behind to Stanley Matthews's Blackpool and twice Jack Rowley levelled, before goals from Stan Pearson and half back John Anderson won the FA Cup.

"I'm very pleased to be taking this cup back to Manchester again after a period of 40 years," United

Captain Johnny Carey is chaired around Wembley after United's victory in their first appearance at the stadium captain Carey declared after receiving the trophy.

They were runners-up in four of the first five seasons after the war, yet the title eluded United, who returned to Old Trafford in August 1949. In his quest to win the Championship, Busby looked increasingly to youth. Half back Jackie Blanchflower, 18, and full back Roger Byrne, 21, made their debuts in a goalless draw at Liverpool in November 1951, and the *Manchester Evening News* talked of United's "Babes" being "cool, confident".

Later in the season, Byrne joined Pearson and Rowley in the forward line, and the lethal trio smashed 59 goals between them to deliver Busby's first title. They celebrated by annihilating Arsenal 6-1 at Old Trafford on the final day of 1951/52.

But failure to defend the title prompted Busby to again refresh his team. Strapping half back Duncan Edwards made his debut at 16, goalscorer Dennis Viollet was promoted from the youth set-up, and forward Tommy Taylor arrived from Barnsley. In 1955/56, young forwards David Pegg and Liam Whelan, and half back Mark Jones, became first-team regulars as the team, now captained by Roger Byrne, won the title by a massive 11 points. The Taylor-Viollet combination yielded 47 goals.

United's first European Cup campaign formed part of a classic season in which they retained the title, with three games to spare, and were runners-up in the FA Cup. The European adventure included the 10-0 destruction of Anderlecht, still the club's record win, and it took Real Madrid, the cup holders and eventual winners, to halt United's

A haunting image of the Busby Babes before the game against Red Star in Belgrade in 1958. Eight of the players would perish on the flight home

Matt Busby urges one last push as the 1968 European Cup final goes to extra time

progress in the semi-finals. The Busby Babes were coming of age, and more players were graduating from the youth system, like Bobby Charlton, who scored twice on his debut against Charlton Athletic in October 1956.

United's form in the early months of 1957/58 was patchy, but the signs were, after the turn of the year, that they were settling into a good run. On 1st February 1958, they beat Arsenal 5-4 at Highbury – a game often described as the greatest ever played in England. Four days later, a 3-3 draw at Red Star Belgrade secured progress to another European Cup semi-final.

But then the dream team that had thrilled spectators throughout England and Europe was wrecked when the plane carrying these popular young men back to

Manchester crashed in the ice and snow of a Munich afternoon. In all, 23 people, including players, staff, supporters and journalists, perished. Seven players were killed instantly: full backs Geoff Bent and Roger Byrne, half backs Eddie Colman and Mark Jones, forwards David Pegg, Tommy Taylor and Liam Whelan. Duncan Edwards died later in hospital.

While Busby recovered in a Munich hospital, Jimmy Murphy steered a makeshift team that included survivors Bobby Charlton, Bill Foulkes and Harry Gregg to the FA Cup final. There was no shame in their 2-0 defeat to Bolton at Wembley, nor in elimination from the European Cup by AC Milan, or ninth place in the League.

No trophies were won in the four full seasons after Munich, but Busby worked incessantly. Hard-nosed half back Pat Crerand was signed from Celtic. Alongside him, the equally combative Nobby Stiles emerged from the youth system, as did defenders Bill Foulkes and Shay Brennan.

Denis Law came from Torino to partner David Herd, signed from

United with the trophy they had pursued for so long after an emotional night at Wembley

Arsenal, and Charlton was now a top-drawer forward.
But it was full back Noel Cantwell, signed in 1960
from West Ham, who led United out at Wembley to
face Leicester City in the 1963 FA Cup final. Goals
from Law and Herd (two) gave United a 3–1 victory
and their first trophy since Munich.

In 1963/64, United climbed to second in the First

Division and a 17-year-old winger named George Best made his debut. The following season, the forward line was irresistible. Law scored 28 goals, Herd 19, and Best and Charlton 10 each, as United clinched the title by defeating Arsenal 3-1 at Old Trafford in their penultimate match.

England's first European Cup winners

They failed to win a trophy in 1965/66, but the 5-1 Best-inspired demolition of Benfica in Lisbon suggested more glory would soon arrive. Which it did, as the 6-1 thrashing of West Ham wrapped up the 1967 League Championship, the fifth under Busby, with a game to spare.

It was time for another crack at the ultimate prize. A hard-fought semi-final victory over Real Madrid booked United's place in the Wembley final against Benfica. On a night of high drama and emotion, Charlton struck twice, and there were goals for Best and teenage forward Brian Kidd, as United prevailed 4-1 after extra time. Busby's dream of conquering Europe had finally been realised.

KIT PARADE

There were no lightweight breathable synthetic shirts for the Newton Heath players of the late 1870s, who wore moisture-retaining woollen jerseys that weighed them down when it rained. Happily, it was not long before the shirts were made of lighter materials like cotton.

The original Newton Heath kit resembled a jockey's outfit

To modern eyes, the original Heathens kit looks like a jockey's outfit, with its long-sleeved shirts of yellow and green halves, and black socks pulled up over long white trousers. The Heathens used variations of this strip for the first decade and a half of their existence, until John Davies assumed control of the club, changed the name to Manchester United, and introduced the first red shirts.

Ernest Mangnall's men wore red shirts, white shorts and red socks when they completed United's first Football League title triumph in 1908. In the following year's FA Cup final, United and Bristol City were both obliged to change from their customary red. While City chose blue, United switched to white collarless shirts with a big red V extending from the shoulders to the sternum and a Lancashire red rose adorning the left breast. White shorts and black socks completed the ensemble, and United lifted the Cup.

For two decades United wore red home

shirts and changed into white and blue stripes away from home, if required. But after relegation to the Second Division in 1922, they reverted to the white shirts of their 1909 Cup success. These were worn until 1926, when United were back in the top flight.

The home kit of red shirts, white shorts and black socks remained largely unchanged from 1935 to 1959. But United wore deep blue to avoid a colour clash in the 1948 Cup final success against Blackpool. The shirts were complemented by white shorts and blue socks.

United won the FA Cup in 1909 wearing this change strip

From the mid–1950s to the start of the 1970s, the change kit generally consisted of white shirts with red trim around the neck and cuffs, white shorts and white socks. This was worn when United lost the 1957 Cup final to Aston Villa. The scratch team that lost the 1958 final to Bolton, in the aftermath of Munich, wore the traditional home kit. And the team that triumphed over Leicester at Wembley five years later wore red shirts with fashionable round necks, white shorts and red socks. The latter was to avoid clashing with their opponents' stockings.

An all-white change kit was used for most of the 1960s. But United switched to a specially produced all-blue strip for the 1968 European Cup final triumph, when their opponents, Benfica, wore all white instead of their customary red.

The classic home kit from the era of the Busby Babes

The club badge became a fixture on the shirts in 1972/73. By the mid-1970s, the kit's manufacturer, Admiral, had its logo on the shirts and shorts. Quirky twists to the design included striped collars and three black stripes extending the length of one side of the classic white away shirt.

United's kits of the 1980s were manufactured by Adidas, whose first change was to add stripes to the sleeves and sides of the shorts. It was in this simple, yet striking, design that the Reds lifted the 1983 FA Cup, overcoming Brighton in the final.

That year, the club signed up its first shirt sponsor, Sharp, the Japanese electronics firm. At first, for televised matches, they wore shirts with no sponsor's logo because the television companies refused to carry such advertising. When Norman Whiteside's screamer saw

off Everton in the Cup final two years later, the striped
sleeves were gone and instead a white and black band
now ran around the upper arm.

The standard 1980s away kit was white shirts, black
shorts and black or white socks, while an all-blue third
kit was also introduced. But an all-white strip was
worn for the 1990 Cup final, when United
drew 3-3 with Crystal Palace, before they
won the replay in their traditional outfit. All
white was also chosen for the 1991 Cup
Winners' Cup final triumph over Barcelona.
For their next final, the 1992 League
Cup clash with Nottingham
Forest, United sported their
change kit of blue socks,
blue shorts and blue and
white mosaic-effect shirt.
Fortunately, the hideous top didn't prevent
Brian McClair scoring the game's only goal.

As the top flight became the Premier
League, United enlisted Umbro as their
kit manufacturer. The arrangement
spanned ten years, seven different home
kits and 16 change strips, as the club
capitalised financially on their fanatical
worldwide support. Changes included
lace-up collars for the shirts United sported
when winning the Premier League in 1993
and the 1994 Double. By now, the players'
names appeared on their backs.

For the first European
Cup win in 1968,
United wore this
specially produced
all-blue kit

The collars returned to plain black, with no laces, for the next two campaigns, including the 1996 Double. A floppy collar was introduced in 1996 – a surprise given Eric Cantona's penchant for wearing his upturned. Stripes featuring the Umbro logo appeared on the arms of the 1998-2000 red shirts, in which United clinched two legs of the Treble. These stripes, like the collar, were removed for the 2000–2002 shirt, worn as United completed a hat-trick of titles in 2001.

The ill-fated all-grey kit of 1995/96

The change strips in the Umbro era included a yellow and gold third shirt based on the original Newton Heath colours and the awful all-grey of 1995/96. United failed to win in grey and even changed to blue and white stripes halfway through a defeat at Southampton. They stuck with blue and white for the title-clinching match at Middlesbrough, and never wore grey again. A special European kit of red shirts, white shorts and white socks was worn between 1997 and 2000. In this, United lifted the 1999 European Cup.

Sharp's sponsorship ended in 2000, and Vodafone, the telecommunications company, took over until 2006, when they were replaced by American insurance giant AIG. Ahead of the 2002/03 season, the club agreed a £300 million deal for Nike to provide kits for the next 13 years. Four different home kits appeared in the first seven Nike seasons, plus five away kits, including all-black, all-blue and all-white versions, and four third kits.

A replica of the 1958 strip was worn to mark the 50th anniversary of Munich on 10th February 2008, when United lost to Manchester City. As for all finals, a special shirt bearing the name and date of the match was made for the 2008 Champions League final,

A new kit and a new sponsor for 2010/11

when United defeated Chelsea on penalties. They also wore white socks, not black.

The design for the 2009/10 kit drew inspiration from the kit worn during the club's first FA Cup triumph in 1909. A black V was added to the front of the red home shirts, which were complemented by the usual white shorts and black socks. The away kit was all black except for a blue V on the shirts.

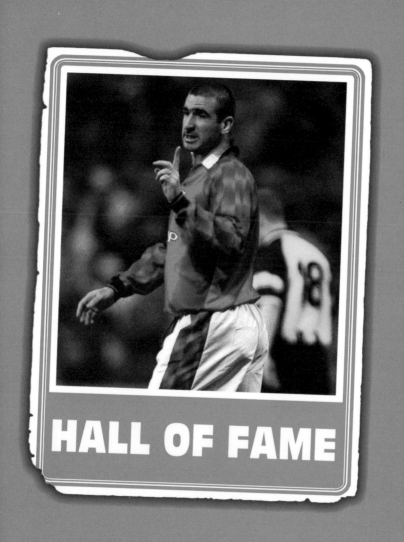

HALL OF FAME

GEORGE BEST

Even on bog-like pitches, with defenders testing his courage to the limit, George Best played with a panache born of sumptuous talent and supreme self-belief.

After making his debut as a skinny 17-year-old against West Brom in September 1963, the Irishman's progress was so rapid that he was a virtual ever-present in the side that won the Championship in 1964/65. Best contributed 10 goals to the title charge as it became clear United had unearthed a truly gifted forward.

His superstar status was confirmed the following season when he inspired United to a memorable triumph at Benfica. Best, still only 19, was dubbed El Beatle by the Portuguese press for a dazzling display. Another League title followed in 1966/67, with Best scoring ten goals.

The next season he was instrumental in the run to the European Cup final, grabbing the only goal of the game in the semi-final first-leg defeat of Real Madrid. In the final, he weaved his way through the Benfica defence to score the extra-time goal that set United on course for glory. Such entrancing performances and 32 goals in the season earned Best the European Footballer of the Year award in July 1968.

"I was on top of the world and it seemed like just the beginning of a long and glorious career," he later recalled.

Best struck over 20 goals in each of the four seasons that followed the European Cup triumph, but this feat only masked United's demise and his personal difficulties. By now, Best was one of football's first pin-ups. He attracted huge media attention, which, as a naturally shy man, he often found hard to handle.

His off-field activities – which included going AWOL, serial womanising and sliding into alcoholism – created tensions between him and the Old Trafford hierarchy. So much so that after a resounding defeat at QPR on New Year's Day 1974, Best left United at the age of just 27. Though he went on to represent many other clubs, he would never again scale the heights to which he rose in the golden days of the 1960s.

> **❝ The complete player. He could ride tackles, hit the ball with either foot, send superb long or short passes ❞**
> Denis Law, team-mate, 1963-73

Born: Belfast, 22nd May, 1946
Died: 25th November 2005
Man Utd appearances: 470
Man Utd goals: 179
Honours won with Man Utd: League title (1965, 67), European Cup (1968)
Other clubs: Dunstable Town (November 1974-November 1975), Stockport County (November 1975-January 1976), Cork Celtic (January-April 1976) Los Angeles Aztecs (April-August 1976), Fulham (September 1976-May 1977), Los Angeles Aztecs (May-August 1977 and March 1978), Fort Lauderdale Strikers (June-August 1978 and March-July 1979) Hibernian (November 1979-April 1980), San Jose Earthquakes (April-August 1980 and March-August 1981), AFC Bournemouth (March-July 1983), Brisbane Lions (July 1983)
International appearances: Northern Ireland, 37; nine goals

GEORGE BEST FACTFILE

ERIC CANTONA

Eric Cantona became a United hero by chance. One afternoon in the autumn of 1992, Leeds United approached their Manchester rivals about buying full back Denis Irwin. The move was rejected, but Alex Ferguson inquired about Cantona. To the manager's surprise, a £1 million transfer was agreed.

It proved the ultimate in inspired moves. Cantona, a Championship winner with Marseille and Leeds, brought a sense of self-belief and destiny that spread through the entire team. "We were an inspired and transformed team," Alex Ferguson later noted. With the flamboyant Cantona operating as a withdrawn striker, United charged to a first title in 26 years.

In 1993/94 came the first Double of the club's history. Cantona, the PFA Player of the Year, coolly converted two penalties in the FA Cup final triumph over Chelsea. United were all set to repeat the feat the following season until Cantona received a lengthy ban for launching himself, kung-fu style, at an abusive Crystal Palace fan in January 1995. It was the latest in a long list of transgressions on either side of the English Channel.

On his return, Cantona played with renewed appetite in

spearheading United's assault on a second Double. In the crucial period between late February and early April 1996, Cantona scored in six consecutive Premier League games, four of which United won 1-0. After helping to secure the Premiership and being named Football Writers' Association Footballer of the Year, his magnificent volley saw off Liverpool in the FA Cup final.

Despite his achievements, Cantona's critics argued that he failed in Europe. In mitigation, he played when United were still learning the hard way against continental opposition. And if some of the chances he created in the 1996/97 Champions League semi-final exit against Borussia Dortmund had been converted, the Reds might well have conquered Europe in his time.

After United retained the Premier League title that season, Cantona decided he'd had enough. A lover of poetry, art and philosophy, Cantona was the antithesis of the typical footballer. Nobody was surprised when he moved into film acting after taking early retirement from football.

> **There are those who represent something extraordinary, something sublime... Eric Cantona belonged in this category**
>
> Peter Schmeichel, team-mate, 1992-1997

Born: Marseille, France, 24th May 1966

Man Utd appearances: 185

Man Utd goals: 82

Honours won with Man Utd: Premier League (1993, 94, 96, 97), FA Cup (1994, 96)

Other clubs: Auxerre (1983-88, including loan to Martigues, September 1985-June 1986), Olympique Marseille (1988-89, including loan to Bordeaux, February-May 1989), Montpellier (1989-90), Olympique Marseille (1990-91), Olympique Nimes (1991-February 1992), Leeds United (February-November 1992)

International appearances: France, 45; 20 goals

ERIC CANTONA FACTFILE

BOBBY CHARLTON

Bobby Charlton embodied the attacking philosophy of the Busby era in an outstanding career that spanned three decades. Whether deployed out wide or in central midfield, his energy, vision and powerful long-range shooting made Charlton truly world-class.

As a 15-year-old he rejected 17 other League clubs to join the United youth system in June 1953. As a 19-year-old Charlton struck ten goals in 14 League appearances as United finished 1956/57 as champions.

By the time United won their European Cup quarter-final against Red Star Belgrade in February 1958, Charlton enjoyed a reputation as one of England's most exciting young forwards. He survived the Munich air crash after being pulled clear of the plane's wreckage by goalkeeper Harry Gregg.

Though the sadness of losing so many friends would remain with him forever, Charlton continued to progress. He made his England debut in April 1958 and smashed 29 goals in 38 League games in 1958/59, operating mainly on the left wing.

Integral to Matt Busby's post-Munich rebuilding, Charlton

soon moved into the centre of midfield, where he could exert greater influence. Two years after helping United to FA Cup glory against Leicester in 1963, he collected his second Championship medal, striking 10 goals in 41 appearances.

By now, Charlton formed part of an attacking trio, alongside George Best and Denis Law, that was the envy of the world. Charlton enjoyed a marvellous 1966, being voted European Footballer of the Year and experiencing World Cup glory with England.

After collecting another League winner's medal in 1967, Charlton captained the side that lifted the European Cup a year later. Charlton bagged a brace as Benfica were defeated in the final. That was to be his last medal, though he spent five more seasons at United before his final match against Chelsea in April 1973.

Charlton has linked different phases of United history as seamlessly as he once linked midfield and attack. He became a club director in 1984 and was knighted a decade later. Only Ryan Giggs has played more times for United, while nobody has scored more goals.

> **The greatest thing for a manager is to trust the talent. Bobby Charlton never betrayed that trust. It was a privilege to have him play for you**
>
> Sir Matt Busby, Charlton's manager, 1956-69

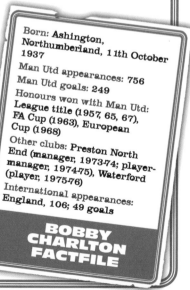

Born: Ashington, Northumberland, 11th October 1937

Man Utd appearances: 756

Man Utd goals: 249

Honours won with Man Utd: League title (1957, 65, 67), FA Cup (1963), European Cup (1968)

Other clubs: Preston North End (manager, 1973-74; player-manager, 1974-75), Waterford (player, 1975-76)

International appearances: England, 106; 49 goals

BOBBY CHARLTON FACTFILE

DUNCAN EDWARDS

No player symbolises the glory and the tragedy of the Busby era like Duncan Edwards. Big Duncan was a footballing colossus who mastered almost every aspect of the game in his short professional career.

Nominally a half back, he was commanding in the air, tough in the tackle, calm in possession, and unleashed a shot so fierce he was nicknamed "Boom Boom" after one 25-yard effort for England against West Germany ended up with goalkeeper and ball in the back of the net. To underline his versatility, Edwards once scored six goals for England under-23s, operating as a centre forward.

Such was Edwards's talent and maturity that Matt Busby gave him his debut at the age of 16. His appearance in the defeat against Cardiff City on 4th April 1953 made Edwards the First Division's youngest-ever player.

Two years later he made his full England debut aged just 18 years and 183 days, meaning Edwards was England's youngest debutant until Michael Owen in February 1998.

In 1955/56, he was a key member of the United team that won the League title, playing 33 times and scoring three goals, despite a bout of influenza that kept him sidelined for almost two months.

The following season he contributed five goals in 34 appearances as United retained the Championship, and was a member of the side that lost the 1957 FA Cup final to Aston Villa.

Edwards was also instrumental in United's run to the semi-finals of their first European Cup campaign, where they lost to Real Madrid.

By February 1958, Edwards and United seemed on course for further glory. But then the team was lost in the Munich air disaster. Even in death, Edwards showed his strength. The 21-year-old fought valiantly for 15 days after the crash before losing his life.

It's hard to compare players from different eras, but astute football men like Bobby Charlton maintain that Edwards was as fine a player as ever wore a United shirt. Charlton once described his friend as "the only player who ever made me feel inferior".

> **❝ His tackling was a series of tank traps, as ferocious as it was perfectly timed; his passing was penetrative and accurate ❞**
>
> Bobby Charlton, Busby Babes team-mate

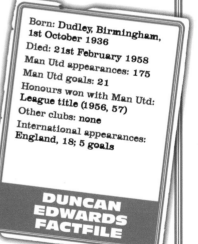

Born: Dudley, Birmingham, 1st October 1936

Died: 21st February 1958

Man Utd appearances: 175

Man Utd goals: 21

Honours won with Man Utd: League title (1956, 57)

Other clubs: none

International appearances: England, 18; 5 goals

DUNCAN EDWARDS FACTFILE

RYAN GIGGS

Giggs was the ultimate teenage prodigy when he burst into the public consciousness, making his debut at the tender age of 17 and cementing his first-team place before turning 19.

The flying winger terrorised defences, striking nine goals in the 1992/93 title triumph and a year later contributing 17 goals and 14 assists to United's first Double.

Such performances earned him the PFA Young Player of the Year award in both 1992 and 1993. By the time the likes of David Beckham and Paul Scholes became first-team regulars in the 1995/96 Double campaign, Giggs was a seasoned pro – at the age of 22.

He continued to mesmerise full backs, giving them what Gary Pallister called "twisted blood", but Giggs also developed a tremendous work ethic, tracking back to aid United's left back.

The Welshman's energy and commitment reached new levels in the 4-0 demolition of Porto in March 1997, when Alex Ferguson deployed him in a deeper, more central role. Giggs scored the third United goal and his overall performance led Ferguson to predict: "In two years he will be a truly wonderful player."

Sure enough, two years later, Giggs produced one of most magical moments in United's history when he slalomed through Arsenal's defence to score the goal that took the Reds to the FA Cup final. Giggs played a full role as United's trophy glut continued in the years that followed the Treble.

However, the man once dubbed the "new George Best" was soon a relatively low-profile member of the team, especially with the celebrity of Beckham and the arrival of big-money signings like Ruud van Nistelrooy, Wayne Rooney and Rio Ferdinand. Always happy to let others have the limelight, Giggs focused on keeping himself in good shape and developing aspects of his game that would help him defy the ageing process.

A series of accomplished displays earned Giggs the 2009 PFA Player of the Year and BBC Sports Personality of the Year awards – personal accolades that were long overdue for a man who has played for United more times than anyone else has. He continued to break new ground in 2010, netting the first league penalties of his career.

❝ I shall always remember my first sight of him, floating over the pitch at the Cliff so effortlessly that you would have sworn his feet weren't touching the ground ❞
Sir Alex Ferguson, manager, 1990-present

Born: Cardiff, 29th November 1973

Man Utd appearances: 838

Man Utd goals: 155

Honours won with Man Utd: Premier League (1993, 94, 96, 97, 99, 2000, 01, 03, 07, 08, 09), FA Cup (1994, 96, 99, 2004), European Champions League (1999, 2008), League Cup (1992, 2006, 09, 10), European Super Cup (1991), Intercontinental Cup (1999), World Club Cup (2008)

Other clubs: none

International appearances: Wales, 64; 12 goals

RYAN GIGGS FACTFILE

ROY KEANE

If ever there was a thankless task, it was the one that faced Roy Keane when he signed from Nottingham Forest for £3.75 million in July 1993. But the Irishman was not daunted by the expectation that he could be Bryan Robson's long-term replacement.

He soon became an Old Trafford favourite, with the fans appreciating his lung-busting determination, robust tackling and ability to score vital goals. Keane's fearsome midfield partnership with the equally pugnacious Paul Ince helped United to the Double in the Irishman's first season.

When Ince left in 1995, Keane relished the mantle of main midfield enforcer. His marauding displays often masked his more subtle abilities, including his fine passing. Tellingly, after winning another Double in 1996 and retaining the Premier League title in 1997, United won nothing when Keane was ruled out by a knee injury for most of 1997/98.

After a long and frustrating period of rehabilitation, Keane returned in August 1998 and, as captain, was the kingpin in that glorious Treble season. The midfielder experienced arguably his finest and most bitter moments against Juventus in the Champions League semi-final. Though he inspired a seemingly impossible comeback, Keane knew he would miss the final after collecting a booking.

The following campaign brought more personal triumphs, including a brace in the 2-1 League win at Arsenal and the only goal of the game as United defeated Palmeiras to lift the Intercontinental Cup. He was also voted PFA Player of the Year, Football Writers' Player of the Year and again lifted the Premier League trophy. Though more trophies followed, Keane would never fulfill his dream of playing in, and winning, a Champions League final.

Even amid such success, his career was littered with controversy, including red cards for unsavoury clashes with the likes of Gareth Southgate, Alf Inge Haaland and Alan Shearer. Nor was Keane ever afraid to speak his mind, once famously vilifying the so-called prawn-sandwich brigade among the Old Trafford crowd. Keane's criticism of United after the 4-1 defeat at Middlesbrough in October 2005 precipitated his departure from Old Trafford.

> ** Keane is an incredible player, a real one-off whose name would be first on the team-sheet of any side **
>
> Jaap Stam, team-mate, 1998-2001

Born: Cork, Republic of Ireland, 10th August 1971

Man Utd appearances: 480

Man Utd goals: 51

Honours won with Man Utd: FA Cup (1994, 96, 99, 2004), Premier League (1994, 96, 97, 99, 2000, 01, 03), European Champions League (1999), Intercontinental Cup (1999)

Other clubs: Nottingham Forest (1990-93), Celtic (December 2005-June 2006)

International appearances: Republic of Ireland, 66; nine goals

ROY KEANE FACTFILE

DENIS LAW

In the summer of 1962, Matt Busby rescued Law, then 22, from a miserable spell in Italy with Torino. The manager told his new forward, who enjoyed coming deep to get involved in approach play, that he would operate as an out-and-out goalscorer alongside target man David Herd.

Shrugging off his initial reluctance to be limited in this way, Law responded by cracking 29 goals in all competitions during his first season at the club, including one in the 1963 FA Cup final. As Busby had realised, the super-confident Aberdonian was the clinical finisher the team needed to complement the attacking verve of Bobby Charlton and the emerging talent of George Best.

In his second season, Law smashed a club record 46 goals in 44 matches, as United came second in the League and enjoyed good runs in the FA and Cup Winners' Cups. Law's outstanding contribution was rewarded when he was named European Footballer of the Year for 1964. The following season, his 30 League goals in as many matches played a major part in securing United's first Division One title of the post-Munich era.

All the while, Law displayed a taste for showmanship. Spectacular volleys and bicycle kicks made him an Old Trafford hero, as did a haul of 23 goals in the title-winning season of 1966/67. "His timing in the air was fantastic. His reflexes on the ground uncanny," said team-mate Pat Crerand.

Sadly for such a pivotal figure in United's success, Law missed out on the greatest night of the club's history. He was in Manchester for a cartilage operation when his colleagues lifted the European Cup in 1968.

In his comeback campaign, Law struck 30 goals, including nine in Europe, but even that was not enough for a successful defence of the European crown. Over the next four seasons, as United deteriorated, Law was unable to reproduce his prolific form of old. In July 1973, he was granted a free transfer to Manchester City.

It is testament to Law's brilliance that he is still known as the King of the Stretford End almost 40 years after his last game for United.

> **" Up there with the all-time greats. Electric. He'd snap up any half chance "**
>
> George Best, team-mate, 1963-73

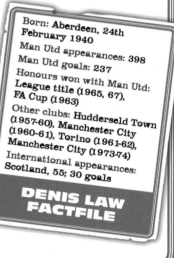

Born: Aberdeen, 24th February 1940

Man Utd appearances: 398

Man Utd goals: 237

Honours won with Man Utd: League title (1965, 67), FA Cup (1963)

Other clubs: Huddersfeld Town (1957-60), Manchester City (1960-61), Torino (1961-62), Manchester City (1973-74)

International appearances: Scotland, 55; 30 goals

DENIS LAW FACTFILE

BRYAN ROBSON

Ron Atkinson rightly described Robson as "pure gold" after signing him for a British record £1.5 million. The archetypal box-to-box midfielder, Robson's all-action style saw him help out in defence, control midfield, and spring forward to score crucial, often spectacular, goals.

Robson's influence seemed limitless. "The pace of the game depended on how quick or slow Bryan Robson wanted to play," team-mate Lee Sharpe recalled. "He controlled their fans, our fans, the referee, both sides."

Within a year of his arrival, Robson was made captain. He responded with 10 League goals as United finished third, though injury robbed him of a first chance to lead out the team at Wembley. In his absence, United lost the 1983 League Cup final narrowly to Liverpool. Robson soon made amends, scoring twice in the FA Cup final replay demolition of Brighton two months later.

The next season, Robson gave what many regard as his greatest performance, scoring twice on a memorable Old Trafford night as United beat Maradona's Barcelona 3-0 in the Cup-Winners' Cup, thus overturning a 2-0 first-leg deficit.

In the successful 1985 FA Cup campaign, Robson's spectacular strike helped defeat Liverpool in the semi-final replay. Confidence was high after another FA Cup triumph and United began 1985/86 in stunning form, with ten straight League wins. But then Robson sustained a nasty shoulder injury, and the team's title challenge soon faded.

Shoulder problems also limited his involvement in the 1986 World Cup. Throughout his career, Robson's combative approach took its toll. Captain Marvel, as England manager Bobby Robson called him, broke or dislocated over 20 bones in his body during his playing days.

Four years later, Robson was the fulcrum of the side that secured the FA Cup, the first silverware under Alex Ferguson. European glory followed a year later when Barcelona were beaten in the Cup Winners' Cup final on a wonderful night in Rotterdam.

Mounting injuries, plus the ageing process, limited his appearances in the title-winning years of 1993 and 1994. Yet Robson still contributed, and lifted the trophy on both occasions.

❝ He was a miracle of commitment, a human marvel who could push himself beyond every imaginable limit on the field ❞

Alex Ferguson, Robson's manager, 1986-94

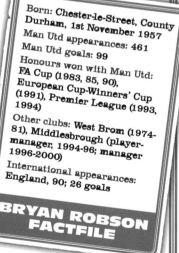

Born: Chester-le-Street, County Durham, 1st November 1957

Man Utd appearances: 461

Man Utd goals: 99

Honours won with Man Utd:
FA Cup (1983, 85, 90), European Cup-Winners' Cup (1991), Premier League (1993, 1994)

Other clubs: West Brom (1974-81), Middlesbrough (player-manager, 1994-96; manager 1996-2000)

International appearances: England, 90; 26 goals

BRYAN ROBSON FACTFILE

CRISTIANO RONALDO

It seemed a strange decision to give the number seven shirt once worn by David Beckham and Eric Cantona, among other Old Trafford greats, to a teenage Portuguese winger. Few United fans had even heard of Cristiano Ronaldo dos Santos Aveiro when he was signed as Beckham's replacement shortly before the 2003/04 campaign kicked off.

But the scepticism vanished when Ronaldo's pace and trickery lit up Old Trafford and his man-of-the-match display in the FA Cup final triumph over Millwall proved that he had a major role to play in United's future. The Portuguese winger was at the heart of Sir Alex Ferguson's strategy to create a young side whose main attributes were pace, energy and versatility. The plan came to fruition when Ronaldo struck 17 league goals in 2006/07 to help deliver United's first title for four years.

The term "world-class" is serially overused, yet it applies to Ronaldo's impact in 2007/08, when he plundered a gobsmacking 42 goals in all competitions. The highlights included his first Premier League hat-trick, against Newcastle and a towering header against Chelsea in the Champions

League final, as United achieved domestic and European glory.

Ronaldo's contribution was recognised when he became the first United player since George Best to be named European Footballer of the Year and the only United player to be voted World Player of the Year. But his summertime flirtations with Real Madrid dented his popularity with many United fans and, troubled by injury, he cut a frustrated figure in the early months of 2008/09.

Ronaldo failed to score between late November and mid-January, before a prolific spell that kick-started United's Premier League and European campaigns. Doubles against Aston Villa and Tottenham helped rescue three points when United were on the verge of catastrophe. Meanwhile, Ronaldo's ability to excel in a variety of roles – on either wing, as a lone striker, or in a front two – made him an increasingly dangerous opponent. As Arsenal discovered in the Champions League semi-final second leg, when Ronaldo tortured them with two superb goals.

> **Ronaldo's speed is amazing. He's so quick. His speed with the ball is the real asset he has. He's probably just as quick running with the ball as he is without it**
>
> Sir Alex Ferguson, Ronaldo's manager, 2003-2009

Born: Madeira, Portugal, 5th February 1985
Man Utd appearances 291
Man Utd goals: 118
Honours won with Man Utd: Premier League (2007, 08, 2009), FA Cup (2004), European Champions League (2008), League Cup (2006, 09), World Club Cup (2008)
Other clubs: Sporting Lisbon (2001-03), Real Madrid (2009-)
International appearances: Portugal, 58; 21 goals

CRISTIANO RONALDO FACTFILE

WAYNE ROONEY

On an unforgettable night in September 2004, it took 19-year-old Wayne Rooney less than an hour to show why Sir Alex Ferguson had spent £25 million to prise him away from Everton.

The striker, who had excelled for England at Euro 2004, smashed an exhilarating hat-trick in the 6-2 Champions League mauling of Fenerbahçe. Rarely has a major signing performed with such freedom and audacity on their debut. But then, as David Beckham once said, Rooney plays every game with the enthusiasm of a child in the back garden. His reward for scoring 17 goals in his first season at Old Trafford was to be named PFA Young Player of the Year, an accolade he retained in 2006. Also in 2006, he won his first senior silverware, scoring twice in the League Cup final trouncing of Wigan.

Few players match Rooney's combination of relentless running and exquisite touch. In 2006/07, he starred in the first of a hat-trick of title triumphs, notching 20 goals in a season for the first time.

But, in terms of goalscoring and creativity, Rooney lived in Cristiano Ronaldo's shadow for the next two seasons, as United dominated the Premiership and in 2008 won the Champions League.

The Englishman was often deployed on the flank to allow Ronaldo to act as the spearhead, a tactic that made the most of Rooney's energy but stymied his attacking talents. Still, Rooney cracked 37 goals in the two campaigns and coolly slotted the goal that made United World Club champions in December 2008.

After Ronaldo's departure, he blossomed as the fulcrum of the attack and displayed the predatory instincts of a top-class finisher, even excelling in the air. A tally of 34 goals in 2009/10 was the highest of his professional career and included winners in the League Cup semi-final and final, four against Hull in the League, and a brace in the thrilling Champions League victory at AC Milan.

Only when he was injured late in the campaign did United's title and European hopes fade, but Rooney deservedly won both the PFA and the Football Writers' Association Player of the Year awards.

> **" He has great control and a great shot with both feet. He scares defenders "**
>
> David Beckham, ex-United star and England team-mate, 2003-09

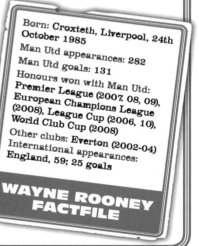

Born: Croxteth, Liverpool, 24th October 1985

Man Utd appearances: 282

Man Utd goals: 131

Honours won with Man Utd: Premier League (2007, 08, 09), European Champions League (2008), League Cup (2006, 10), World Club Cup (2008)

Other clubs: Everton (2002-04)

International appearances: England, 59; 25 goals

WAYNE ROONEY FACTFILE

MUNICH

The defining event in Manchester United's history is not the winning of a cherished trophy, as is the case for most clubs, but the tragic loss of a generation of brilliant young footballers. Eight of Matt Busby's Babes died when the plane carrying the team back to England from a European Cup encounter at Red Star Belgrade crashed in Munich on the wintry afternoon of 6th February 1958.

The English champions' 3-3 draw in Belgrade had secured a semi-final showdown with AC Milan, as United's debut European Cup campaign seemed destined for a glorious finale. But the club's charter plane, an Elizabethan, struggled to take off again after stopping in Munich to refuel. Two attempted take-offs were aborted because of technical problems.

By the time the third attempt began, the mood in the cabin had changed from one of quiet satisfaction to deep concern. "As soon as we started to take off, we thought there was something wrong," Bill Foulkes remembered.

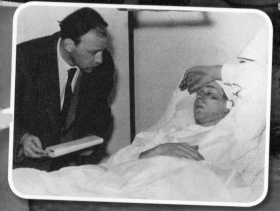

Recovering in hospital, Bobby Charlton talks to a journalist

The plane hit slush towards the end of the runway, then crashed through a fence and crossed a road. One of its wings smashed off after connecting with a house. "The plane slewed and just stopped, nose-dived. We should never have taken off. Never," Foulkes added.

Twenty-one of the 44 passengers and crew died instantly; two more, including Duncan Edwards, passed away later. Survivors such as Bobby Charlton were dragged clear, many by the heroic Harry Gregg. Those who died in the crash, or as a result of injuries sustained in it, included a pilot, journalists, fans and members of the public.

News of the crash stunned the world and took sport to the front pages

The United deceased were: Geoff Bent (full back, aged 25), Roger Byrne (full back, 28), Eddie Colman (half back, 21), Duncan Edwards (half back, 22), Mark Jones (half back, 24), David Pegg (forward, 22), Tommy Taylor (forward, 26), Liam Whelan (forward, 22), Walter Crickmer (secretary, age unknown), Tom Curry (trainer, 64), and Bert Whalley (coach, 45).

Of the injured, Busby was twice read the last rites as he fought for his life in the Munich hospital where he stayed for 71 days. Forwards Johnny Berry and Jackie Blanchflower were so badly injured that they never played again.

The disaster was major news worldwide. "Soccer Air Tragedy," read the front page of the *Daily Mirror*. A huge outpouring of public sympathy accompanied the private grief of the families and friends of the victims, and everyone connected with Old Trafford. Two-minute silences were held at every English football match the following Saturday.

The loss of life was rendered yet more piteous by the fact that so many possibilities died with those young men. "It was one of the greatest tragedies in sport simply because this great team was on the threshold of being the best," said Charlton half a century later.

Within a fortnight of the catastrophe, almost 60,000 spectators crammed into Old Trafford to see a makeshift side, captained by Foulkes and managed by Jimmy Murphy, beat Sheffield Wednesday 3-0 in the FA Cup. Remarkably, United reached the Cup final, but lost to Bolton. Unsurprisingly, they exited the European Cup and slipped to ninth in the League. At the end of the season, UEFA invited United to enter the 1958/59 European Cup, as a tribute to the fallen. Inexplicably, the Football Association vetoed the proposal.

Only after persuasion from his wife, Jean, did Busby return to work. The manager blamed himself for the loss of his players and colleagues, since United had entered European competition at his insistence. "Deep down the sorrow is there all the time," he once revealed. "You never really rid yourself of it. It becomes part of you."

It took Busby five years to build another team capable of gaining honours. After winning the FA Cup in 1963 and the League in 1965 and 1967, United finally scaled the heights Busby had targeted when he first took them into Europe. "When we won, I felt sadness," Foulkes later recalled of the 1968 European Cup triumph. "My thoughts were with the boys who died. The night before the final we had a meeting

50 years on, the
fallen have not
been forgotten

and agreed we had to win it for them."

Today Munich is permanently commemorated at Old
Trafford, by the Munich Clock, which bears the date of
the crash, a plaque with the names of the dead, and the
renaming of the old tunnel as the Munich Tunnel. The 40th
anniversary of the disaster was marked by a benefit match
for the families of the victims, which doubled as a farewell
for Eric Cantona, who had left United the previous year.
Although each of the families reportedly received £47,000
after the game in August 1998, the club has often been
accused of not doing enough to support them.

For the 50th anniversary, a memorial service was held at
Old Trafford on 6th February 2008. United wore a replica of
the 1958 strip when they entertained Manchester City four
days later. And the manager, Sir Alex Ferguson, described
why Munich should always be remembered: "Because
the origins of this football club, as it is today, go back to
that time."

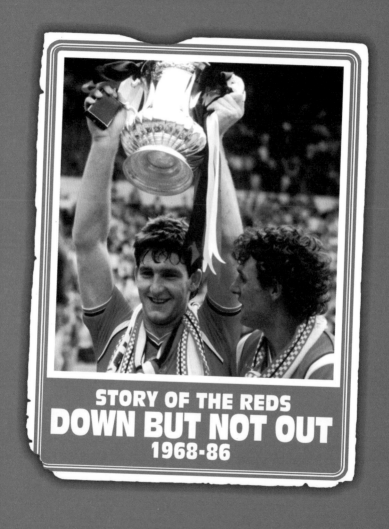

STORY OF THE REDS
DOWN BUT NOT OUT
1968-86

The descent into oblivion was as rapid as it was unexpected. In 1968/69, the Reds plummeted to 11th in the League and lost the World Club Championship to Estudiantes de la Plata, an Argentine team of seemingly limitless thuggery.

United's defence of their European crown set up a semi-final showdown with AC Milan. After a 2-0 reverse at a hostile San Siro, over 63,000 spectators packed into Old Trafford, hopeful of a memorable comeback.

It seemed possible when Charlton scored on 70 minutes, but Denis Law was then denied a goal, despite TV pictures suggesting the ball had crossed the line. United were out, while Milan went on to European glory.

During the season Busby, now Sir Matt, announced that he would act as general manager from the following campaign. Youth team coach Wilf McGuinness, who played in the 1957 title-winning team, succeeded Busby as team manager. Young McGuinness found it hard to handle great players, some of whom had been his team-mates. "Being 31 was a handicap," he admitted. "Having grown up with Bobby Charlton, that might have been difficult, especially when I left Bobby and Denis Law out of the team."

McGuinness's ageing side finished eighth in 1969/70 and won just five League games before Christmas 1970, a record so poor that McGuinness was demoted to reserve team coach. Busby took

temporary charge as United finished eighth again and
made no impression in the FA Cup.

On Busby's recommendation, United turned
to Frank O'Farrell, who had just won the Second
Division with Leicester City. By Christmas 1971
United were five points clear at the top of the table,
then won just nine League games in the next year.
O'Farrell was sacked after a 5-0 thrashing at Crystal
Palace in December 1972. Like McGuinness, he had
been unable to escape the shadow of Busby, now a
club director.

O'Farrell's replacement, the colourful Scotland
manager Tommy Docherty, faced a big rebuilding job.

Fans mob Denis Law
after the game that sent
United down in 1974

"The club was in a terrible state," he later revealed. "It needed about 16 players." The Doc steered United to safety in 1972/73, after which Charlton retired, aged 36. Law, now 33, was given a free transfer to Manchester City, and halfway through the following campaign Best also left. Sadly, his rock star lifestyle was wrecking his footballing genius.

Impish forward Lou Macari arrived from Celtic and sturdy full back Stewart Houston from Brentford, but the rapid churn of players made consistency almost impossible. An agonising defeat to Manchester City in April 1974, when Denis Law back-heeled the game's only goal, condemned United to relegation.

Docherty's reconstruction programme included spending £200,000 on Hull City striker Stuart Pearson, whose 16 goals led United to the Second Division title. Home crowds of never less than 40,000 witnessed a resurgence that was also aided by the defensive steel of Martin Buchan, the midfield energy of Sammy McIlroy and 11 goals from winger Gerry Daly.

Back in the First Division, United finished a creditable third and reached the 1976 FA Cup final against Second Division Southampton, where they lost to a Bobby Stokes goal. Docherty told his players: "We'll be back here again next year."

United slipped to sixth in 1977, but Docherty's Wembley prediction came true. The clash with Liverpool was decided in a few frenetic second-half minutes. Pearson's drive put United ahead, but Jimmy Case soon equalised. Then Macari smashed a shot that,

Jimmys Nicholl and Greenhoff help Alex Stepney show off the 1977 FA Cup he later joked, was bound for Wembley Central until it deflected off Jimmy Greenhoff's chest into the net.

"We've brought the Cup back to the finest supporters in the world," Docherty declared on the triumphant return to Manchester. But news soon broke of Docherty's affair with Mary Brown, the wife of the club's physiotherapist, and Docherty was fired.

Mild-mannered Dave Sexton came from QPR with a reputation for technical expertise. He invested almost £1 million in Leeds centre half Gordon McQueen and striker Joe Jordan, yet United finished eighth and failed in the Cups.

A place in the 1979 FA Cup final was some consolation for another poor League campaign. In an extraordinary match, United were two goals down with five minutes left. As hope faded, McQueen and McIlroy struck to bring United level, only for Arsenal to find a winner seconds from time.

Under mounting pressure to deliver silverware, Sexton bought Chelsea's Ray Wilkins, for his midfield craft. Six consecutive wins in the 1979/80 run-in gave United hope of overtaking leaders Liverpool until they fell to Leeds at the last.

In January 1980, a TV documentary accused Louis Edwards, United's chairman since 1965, of corruption. Edwards denied the claims but died of a sudden heart attack before he could clear his name. His son, Martin, became chairman and approved the club record £1.25 million signing of striker Garry Birtles. Amazingly, Birtles, so prolific for Nottingham

Forest, failed to score a League goal in 1980/81. United slid to eighth, and Sexton was dismissed.

Believing a big personality would bring success, Edwards appointed Ron Atkinson, who had guided West Brom into Division One. Atkinson splashed a record £1.5 million on dynamic West Brom midfielder Bryan Robson, and United finished third

Bryan Robson signs in October 1981 as Ron Atkinson and Martin Edwards look on

two seasons running. Meanwhile, the pain of losing
the 1983 League Cup final to Liverpool was soon
extinguished by another trip to Wembley.

United survived plenty of scares in a 2-2 draw
with Brighton. In the replay, Robson's crisp strike

settled the nerves before striker Norman Whiteside's header doubled the lead. That goal made Belfast-born Whiteside the youngest player to score in an FA Cup final, at 18 years and 18 days. Robson struck again and Dutch midfielder Arnold Muhren converted a second-half penalty to secure United's first trophy for six years.

FA Cup victory in 1985 was Ron Atkinson's side's finest hour

After two fourth-place finishes, Atkinson's finest hour came in the 1985 FA Cup final against champions Everton. A tense encounter went into extra time, with United a man light after Kevin Moran's red card, before Whiteside struck an exquisite winner.

When United won their first 10 fixtures of 1985/86, it seemed the agonising 19-year wait for a League title was over. But after being 10 points clear in October, they crumbled and won only 12 of the remaining 32 games. The capitulation, and six defeats in the first 13 games of the next season, cost Atkinson his job.

TACTICS

BUSBY'S TRINITY

By the 1960s, most English teams had discarded the traditional all-out-attack formation of two full backs, three half backs and five forwards for a more pragmatic 4-4-2 or 4-3-3.

Busby often preferred 4-3-3. But this could be adapted to meet the specific challenges of the opposition and the match situation. For instance, Busby provided greater protection for the defence by instructing his men to play 4-4-2 for tricky away games, especially in Europe. However, that could quickly be changed to 4-2-4 when they were attacking, chasing the game, or against inferior opposition.

In a 4-3-3 formation, the wingers, George Best and John Aston Junior for most of 1967/68, would work the flanks either side of the centre forward, Denis Law. When the ball was on the opposite flank, the other winger would move into the centre to support Law.

Law was also supported by Bobby Charlton, who would spring forward from midfield. So that United didn't become exposed, two holding players, usually Pat Crerand and Nobby Stiles, anchored the midfield in Charlton's absence.

The use of quick, nimble wingers allowed Busby's teams to maintain their manager's attacking philosophy without sacrificing defensive solidity or midfield control. In the example shown, Best would cross for Law to score. This sort of move had plenty of other permutations. Law might lay the ball back for Charlton to shoot, or the winger could square for Charlton to run onto the ball on the edge of the box.

Busby's so-called Trinity was irresistible. Law was a ruthless marksman, Best's pace and trickery could rip a team apart, and Charlton controlled the tempo of United's play and came from deep to score crucial goals. Happy days.

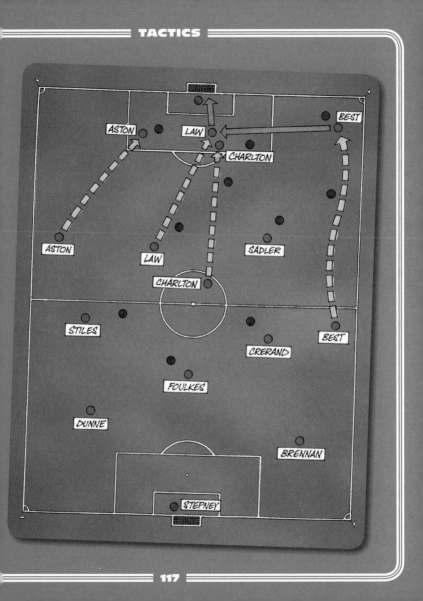

FERGIE'S FLYING WINGERS

As well as being an outstanding last line of defence, Peter Schmeichel often launched United's lightning counter-attacks. This approach was at its most devastating between 1992 and 1995, as United became experts in transforming defence into attack.

The goalkeeper would gather the ball at an opposition set-piece and quickly bowl it out to one of the wingers, Lee Sharpe, Ryan Giggs or Andrei Kanchelskis. In an instant, United's opponents were exposed, their midfield taken out of the game by Schmeichel's rapid distribution. One of the defenders left on the halfway line would have to move across to try and challenge United's winger, and this would create space through the middle.

The United winger would carry the ball at great pace into the opponents' half before looking to cross for the likes of Mark Hughes, Eric Cantona and Andy Cole to convert. The tactic was simplicity itself, yet deadly efficient. And it continued Old Trafford's tradition of attacking football, with Ferguson's men looking to turn every defensive situation into an offensive move.

On other occasions, Schmeichel would hurl the ball straight up towards the centre spot, where Mark Hughes, an expert at holding up play, would retain possession, back to goal, until he could release one of the wingers or play the ball into the path of a supporting player, like Cantona or midfielder Roy Keane. Again, it was simple, but the key was having players who were adept at fulfilling the different roles within the plan.

And Fergie's flying wingers weren't just providers, they were goalscorers. In the Double season of 1993/94, Giggs, Kanchelskis and Sharpe contributed 38 goals between them in all competitions.

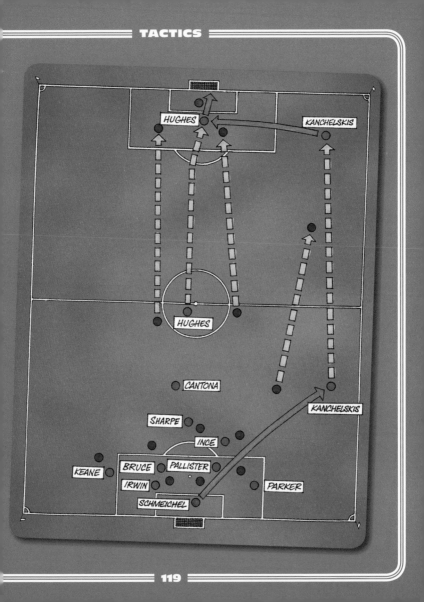

EXPLOITING BECKHAM'S CROSSING

When Andrei Kanchelskis was sold to Everton in the summer of 1995, many United fans feared the team would miss his electric pace on the wing. His replacement, David Beckham, lacked the Ukrainian's speed but offered other important qualities. Soon after Beckham became a first team fixture in 1996, it became clear that his crossing was one of United's principal weapons.

Unlike a traditional winger, Beckham could cross the ball accurately and with pace without having to first beat the full back marking him. The key was to work the ball out to Beckham on the right flank so that he could then deliver crosses for the likes of Andy Cole, Dwight Yorke and Paul Scholes to attack.

In the example shown, Roy Keane has the ball in midfield and releases Gary Neville, sprinting forward from right back. By making the extra man, Neville allows Beckham more space. Neville then passes to Beckham and offers the overlap, at which point Beckham can cross, return the ball to Neville, or even switch play to Ryan Giggs on the left flank. In the diagram, he crosses and Yorke scores.

Having played together through United's youth ranks, Beckham and Neville had an intuitive understanding, so that Neville, blessed with greater pace, would sometimes overlap and deliver the final ball.

Beckham's crosses were the source of numerous goals in the Treble season, including both Yorke's goals in the Champions League quarter-final first leg defeat of Internazionale. In the second leg, however, with Beckham well marshalled, it was Neville's cross from the right that was knocked down by Andy Cole for Paul Scholes to score.

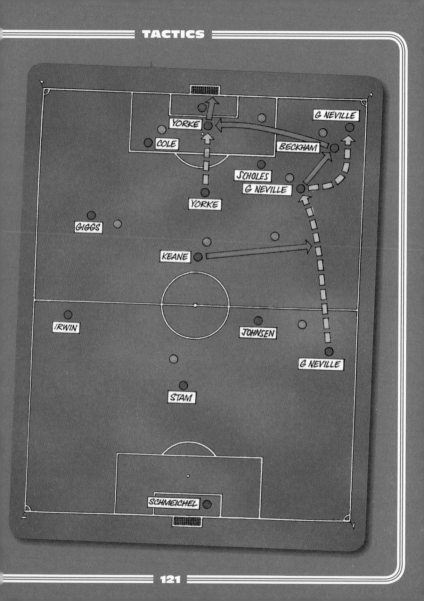

THE WITHDRAWN STRIKER

United have used variations of the split-striker system since Eric Cantona's arrival in 1992. Others who have played this role include Teddy Sheringham, Wayne Rooney and Dimitar Berbatov.

In a traditional 4-4-2, where the strikers play close together, the ball often travels to them in the air where they struggle to match the strength of opposing centre halves. Even if the striker does beat the defender in the air, it is hard for him to head the ball on to a team-mate. Or, if the ball comes along the ground, it is hard for the striker receiving it to find his partner, whose marker is in close attention.

But, as Cantona showed so expertly, if one striker drops off, he can create a link between midfield and attack so that the ball can travel to feet. This also creates a problem for the opposing centre halves: does one of them step forward and mark the withdrawn striker, creating the risk that the attacking side will exploit the space behind him, or stay where he is and become redundant?

Cantona made the no-man's land between the opponents' defence and midfield his own. In the diagram, the ball is played up to the centre forward, Mark Hughes or Andy Cole, who lays it off to Cantona. Unmarked, the Frenchman now has many options. With the wingers bursting forward either side of him and the centre forward distracting the opposing centre halves, Cantona can pass, dribble or shoot.

This approach gave Cantona, and those who followed in later years, freedom to weave his magic wherever he perceived a weak point in the opposing defence. It also allows the withdrawn striker, normally someone who is a good passer and blessed with great vision, to drop into midfield and influence the play, a role in which Berbatov was often used in 2008/09.

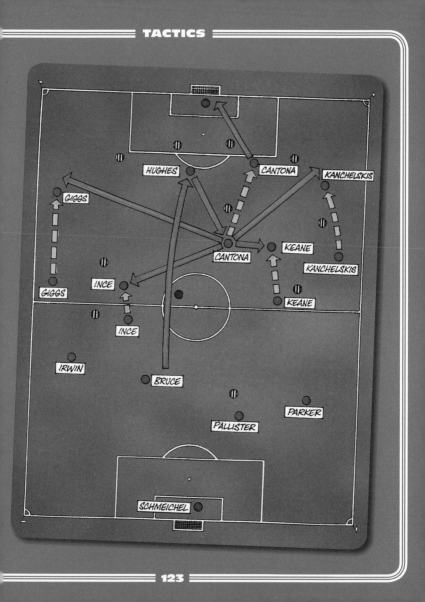

GREAT
GAFFERS

For all United's stature and celebrity, they have had remarkably few great managers. Only three United bosses have won England's top flight, which must be considered the minimum criterion for greatness. Even more surprising is how much time elapsed between the trophy-laden eras of Ernest Mangnall (1903-1912), Matt Busby (1945-1969) and Alex Ferguson (1986-present).

United in 1905, with a bowler-hatted Ernest Mangnall

When Mangnall was appointed in September 1903, his remit included scouting and signing new players and training and coaching the team. Within three seasons, he forged a side that earned promotion to the First Division. The manager then pulled off a stunning transfer coup that brought in several top-quality performers, including star winger Billy Meredith, from Manchester City. The injection of class and experience helped United to their first-ever League Championship in 1908. A first FA Cup triumph came a year later.

Although some of his methods were strange – he rarely allowed the players to use the ball in training – Mangnall oversaw the first golden period of United's history. In the next two seasons, the club moved to its new home, Old Trafford, and Mangnall's men again finished top of the League. But in the following campaign, 1911/12, United slumped to 13th. The team was ageing and began to break up. The manager left, too, for Manchester City.

Like Mangnall, Matt Busby was afforded unprecedented powers concerning team affairs after becoming United boss in 1945. Busby saw that in order to build a side with the skills and ethos he wanted, he needed to identify and nurture local talent, recruit carefully selected targets from other clubs and engender in the players his philosophy of attacking football.

Matt Busby in 1928, while a player at Manchester City

Busby energised the players, donning a tracksuit and joining them in training to impart his ideas. He was a first-class man manager but preferred not to overload his players with the nuances of different tactics. Often, his team talk simply consisted of: "Go out and enjoy yourselves."

The Busby approach soon bore fruit as United secured the 1948 FA Cup. Nevertheless, Busby realised that his team needed refreshing if further trophies were to be won. Older players were replaced by graduates from the junior ranks, such as Roger Byrne. Byrne made a major contribution to the 1951/52 title triumph, scoring seven times in United's last six games.

Determined to avoid

Busby on the training ground in 1957

complacency, Busby introduced more home-grown youngsters, including the redoubtable Duncan Edwards. Half the members of the title-winning sides of 1956 and 1957 had been promoted from the youth system. With so much talent at his disposal, Busby's ambitions spread to Europe. But it was during United's first European Cup campaign, in 1957/58, that eight of Busby's team died in the Munich air disaster.

The trauma of Munich and his own near-death experience did not deter Busby from his rebuilding mission. "Even after Munich, we had to go on, if only out of respect for those who had perished in the cause of Manchester United," he said. Again Busby relied on a productive youth system and his transfer market savvy to provide the players required. But it was a slow process. Only in the fifth season after Munich did United capture another trophy, the 1963 FA Cup.

Two years later, with Bobby Charlton, Denis Law and George Best now in full flow, Busby celebrated his fourth title. The fifth followed in 1967, before Busby's dream of lifting the European Cup was finally realised. He relinquished the manager's role a year later, in May 1969. Busby later became a board member and club president, a position he held until his death in January 1994.

Busby's original aim was to transform United from an underachieving medium-size club into a genuine big hitter. The extent to which he succeeded is evidenced by the fact that his statue now stands outside Old Trafford and United's fans still sing his name.

Busby's United were the first English team to lift the European Cup

After replacing Ron Atkinson in November 1986, Alex Ferguson's intention was to "knock Liverpool off their perch". He wanted to make United England's premier club, just as he had broken the Celtic-Rangers duopoly of the Scottish title with Aberdeen.

Major surgery was required to revive the fortunes of a club that had not won the League for almost two decades. New players were signed, old ones offloaded and Ferguson eradicated deep-seated bad habits like the drinking culture that he believed harmed the players' performance.

The transition was painful. United fans endured sterile football and results so poor that only the 1990 FA Cup triumph saved Fergie's job. His decision to replace goalkeeper Jim Leighton with Les Sealey for the replay proved he had the ruthlessness to succeed. A 1-0 victory over Crystal Palace vindicated the selection and opened the door for almost two decades of sustained success.

In 1993, the first of 11 Premier League titles was secured. A glut of other trophies included four more FA Cups and two Champions League triumphs. The 2009 Premier League triumph saw United equal Liverpool's record of 18 top-flight titles.

Generations of players have reflected Ferguson's unquenchable desire for success. "Alex Ferguson was the perfect manager for me," Roy Keane once said. "He was dedicated and hungry." And anyone who has failed to meet the manager's high standards has received the infamous Ferguson hairdryer treatment.

For someone of such unshakeable beliefs, Ferguson is highly adept at managing change. He has built three truly great sides: the 1994 Double winners of Eric Cantona and co; the 1999 Treble side, led by Roy Keane; and the Rooney-Ronaldo team that won a hat-trick of titles between 2007 and 2009 and the Champions

In 1986, a new manager was introduced to the club's fans...

League in 2008. Each has developed a style of play to suit the demands of its era, while maintaining the tradition of attractive attacking football.

Ferguson is unrelentingly hard-nosed and an expert at manipulating the media. He gets under the skin of rival managers and has drawn memorable outbursts from the likes of Newcastle's Kevin Keegan and Liverpool's Rafa Benítez. Though he is loyal to his players, Ferguson is never sentimental. Hence selling the likes of Paul Ince, David Beckham, Jaap Stam and Ruud van Nistelrooy. Only with Stam was he wrong to think that the player had already given his best years to United.

...Alex Ferguson, pictured with the World Club trophy in 2008, has gone on to be the club's greatest gaffer

For sheer weight of trophies Ferguson, knighted after guiding United to the Treble in 1999, is United's greatest manager. He is also the most successful manager in the history of English football, with 26 major honours to his name. But the biggest single achievement by a United boss was Busby's rebuilding of his team after the impact of Munich, something he did with inimitable style and humility.

The managers who succeeded Mangnall and Busby found it impossible to emulate the feats of the men they replaced. Somebody will one day have the impossible task of taking over from Sir Alex Ferguson.

Daily Mirror **CHAMPS!**

5d Thursday, May 30, 1968 ★ No. 20,029

I'm the proudest man in England,

says Matt Busby

FROM NOBBY TO
BOBBY-THE GRIN
THAT SAYS: IT'S
OURS AT LAST

MEMORABLE MATCHES

MANCHESTER UNITED 4
BENFICA 1

European Cup final, Wembley Stadium, London, 29th May 1968

Ten years on from Munich, United had the chance to pay a special tribute to the fallen by becoming the first English club to lift the European Cup. Benfica, playing in their fifth final, stood between United and the realisation of the dream that had driven Matt Busby to take his side into Europe.

The Portuguese giants, who included legends like skipper Mario Coluna and centre forward Eusebio, would prove tough opponents. And despite home advantage, United's task was rendered more difficult by the absence, through injury, of the prolific Denis Law.

But as Bobby Charlton, the United captain, said later, "we had come too far and had been through too much for us to fail in that final match".

Busby's men started brightly, with John Aston Jr. flying forward on the left flank. On the right, however, George Best was shackled by a series of savage challenges. United created openings, yet Benfica went closest as Eusebio's fierce drive struck Alex Stepney's crossbar. "Keep doing what you're doing, boys. Be patient, keep passing," ordered Busby at half time.

Eight minutes into the second period, David Sadler whipped in a cross from the left and Charlton rose, unmarked, to flick a header beyond goalkeeper Jose Henrique. Several times United almost doubled their lead, only for Jaime Graça to volley the equaliser 15 minutes from time. Eusebio then had the chance to break United hearts, but cracked his shot straight at Stepney.

Bobby Charlton exchanges pennants with Mario Coluna at kick-off

"Let's stop giving the ball away," Busby cajoled at the end of normal time. "Let's get hold of it and keep it and make them do all the running."

Both sides were leg-weary because of the humidity of the night and the energy-sapping lushness of the Wembley turf. But in the opening minutes of extra time Best, socks around his ankles, nutmegged centre-half Fernando Cruz, danced around Henrique, and walked the ball home. A minute later Brian Kidd, Law's teenage replacement, headed the third. And Charlton soon completed the rout with a rasping drive.

After the final whistle came an outpouring of emotion as intense as any seen in a sporting arena. "Winning the European Cup had been a duty to Manchester United," Charlton recalled.

United:
Stepney; Brennan, Foulkes, Stiles, A Dunne; Crerand, Charlton, Sadler; Best, Kidd, Aston Jr.

Scorers:
Charlton (2), Best, Kidd

Attendance:
100,000

MANCHESTER UNITED 1 EVERTON 0

FA Cup final, Wembley Stadium, London, 18th May 1985

Although United had won the FA Cup two years earlier, they were underdogs against an Everton side on course for an unprecedented treble after winning the League and European Cup-Winners' Cup. Yet, in a game of few chances, United matched the favourites blow for blow.

Then, with 12 minutes left, Everton's Peter Reid latched onto a wayward pass by centre half Paul McGrath and sprinted towards Gary Bailey's goal. United's other central defender, Kevin Moran, launched himself into a desperate challenge that missed the ball and sent Reid tumbling. Moran was deemed by referee Peter Willis to have committed a professional foul that denied a goalscoring opportunity. His punishment was a red card.

United's players confront the ref after Kevin Moran is sent off

As a dejected Moran trudged from the field, the first man to be dismissed in an FA Cup final, Ron Atkinson rearranged his ten men. Striker Frank Stapleton

switched to centre half, in Moran's place, leaving Mark Hughes up front on his own.

United's task of surviving almost 45 minutes of normal and extra time to earn a replay seemed an impossible one, especially against a team that had thrashed them 5-0 earlier in the campaign. But the Reds were inspired. They continued to press and harry Everton.

With only ten more minutes left to survive, Hughes relieved the pressure by releasing Norman Whiteside on the right flank, halfway inside the Everton half. "I was stuck out on the right wing, getting back from the attack before. I was absolutely knackered," Whiteside admitted later.

The Irishman lacked support and was faced by ample defensive cover, yet he strode purposefully into the penalty area, ingeniously using defender Pat van den Hauwe to shield the ball from the view of goalkeeper Neville Southall.

Southall, one of Europe's foremost shot-stoppers, was unsighted as Whiteside unleashed a delicious curling left-foot shot that fizzed beyond the keeper's despairing grasp into the far corner of the net. "I used the defender as a screen to buy that extra yard so that Neville couldn't get to it," Whiteside recalled.

Valiantly, the Reds saw out the final few minutes before celebrating their improbable victory.

United:
Bailey; Gidman, McGrath, Moran, Albiston (Duxbury); Olsen, Robson, Strachan, Whiteside; Hughes, Stapleton

Scorer:
Whiteside

Attendance:
100,000

JUVENTUS 2
MANCHESTER UNITED 3

Champions League semi-final second leg, Stadio Delle Alpi, Turin, 21st April 1999

As if United's task wasn't hard enough after the first leg ended 1-1, giving Juventus the advantage of an away goal, they conceded twice in the opening 11 minutes in Italy. Filippo Inzaghi scored both goals for Juve, whose fans were already celebrating a place in the final.

Sheer ecstasy after Cole bags the winner

But the festivities looked premature when United skipper Roy Keane rose to glance home a David Beckham corner on 24 minutes. And the home fans were stunned to silence ten minutes later when Andy Cole's cross was converted by Dwight Yorke's diving header.

Now the away goals rule favoured the visitors. But the yellow card count did not. The inspirational Keane was cautioned for a foul on Zinedine Zidane, meaning he would miss the final should United get through. The same fate befell Paul Scholes later in the contest. Undeterred, Keane gave a true captain's performance, controlling midfield and breaking up

Juventus attacks so that United could hit the Italians on the break. "It was the most emphatic display of selflessness I have seen on a football field," Alex Ferguson reminisced.

Shortly before the interval, Yorke came agonisingly close to increasing United's advantage, but his firm strike hit Angelo Peruzzi's upright and flew to safety. After half time, Juventus searched for the goal that would swing the tie back in their favour. On came Nicola Amoruso to provide a strike partner for Inzaghi, who had a goal rightly ruled out for offside.

Though United were now on the back foot, they threatened to kill off the game with some electric counter-attacks. At the end of one such move, full back Denis Irwin saw his low shot rebound off the inside of a post. Finally, with six minutes remaining, Yorke broke through on goal and was tripped by Perruzzi. Referee Urs Meier played the advantage, allowing Cole to slide the ball into an empty net.

"It is a very proud moment for me. This is the level we want to play at," Ferguson beamed in the post-match press conference. "My players were absolutely fantastic." A month later, following another astonishing comeback, United lifted the European Cup for the first time in 41 years.

'Juve, the stuff of madness' was the Italian press's take on this extraordinary match

United:
Schmeichel; G Neville, Stam, Johnsen, Irwin; Beckham, Keane, Butt, Blomqvist (Scholes 68); Yorke, Cole

Scorers:
Keane, Yorke, Cole

Attendance:
64,500

NEWCASTLE UNITED 0 MANCHESTER UNITED 1

Premier League, St James' Park,
Newcastle, 4th March 1996

Victory was imperative for United since they trailed leaders Newcastle by four points and had played a game more. Defeat would give the Magpies an almost insurmountable advantage and, perhaps as importantly, the self-belief to storm to a rare title triumph.

Unstoppable Cantona dances through the Newcastle ranks

The home side, managed by Kevin Keegan, had gained a reputation for their fine attacking play and approached the game as if they could win the Premier League there and then. The likes of Peter Beardsley, David Ginola and Faustino Asprilla poured forward, threatening the United goal and creating a series of openings for centre forward Les Ferdinand.

Only the agility and bravery of Peter Schmeichel kept Newcastle at bay, as the goalkeeper twice denied Ferdinand in one-on-ones. "It was almost a miracle that we emerged unscathed from the opening 20 minutes," Alex Ferguson remembered.

"Peter was unbelievable as he thwarted Newcastle time and again."

In United's only attack of the first half, Ryan Giggs saw his shot comfortably blocked by Philippe Albert, who had earlier struck Schmeichel's crossbar with a fierce free kick. United's young side had endured a torrid first period, while Newcastle prospered in front of their deafeningly vociferous fans, who created an atmosphere that Ferguson likened to the "lion's den".

At the break, the manager asked his players if they wanted to win the title as much as Newcastle. Within six minutes of the restart, they gave their answer. Roy Keane seized a loose ball on the United right, after Newcastle had cleared a corner, and fired a crossfield pass to Phil Neville.

The full back drove infield and exchanged passes with Andy Cole on the edge of the box before delivering a looping cross towards the far post. The centre was met by the unmarked Eric Cantona, who drove a low volley into the far corner of the net. "That blow drained the confidence out of our opponents," Ferguson noted.

As Geordie tears flowed, United stood firm to complete a victory that was a major turning point in the title race. "After that defeat, Newcastle were never going to win the Championship," Keane recalled. "It was ours."

United:
Schmeichel; Irwin, Bruce, G Neville, P Neville; Sharpe, Keane, Butt, Giggs; Cantona, Cole.

Scorer:
Cantona

Attendance:
36,584

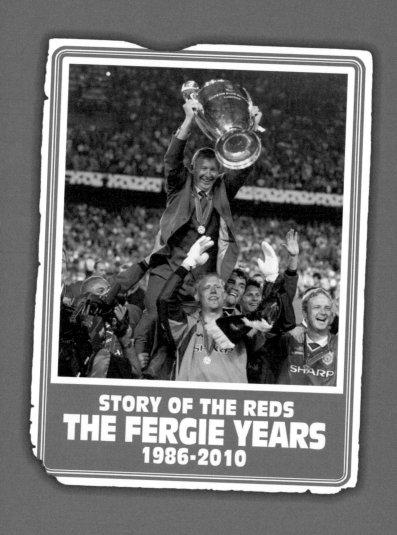

STORY OF THE REDS
THE FERGIE YEARS
1986-2010

For all Alex Ferguson's achievements

at Aberdeen – including three Scottish titles and the European Cup Winners' Cup – his stewardship of United started inauspiciously, with defeat at Oxford United on 8th November 1986.

Mid-table mediocrity in three of Ferguson's first four seasons heaped the pressure on. By January 1990, word was that defeat at Nottingham Forest in the FA Cup would end his tenure. Happily, striker Mark Robins headed the tie's only goal to begin a run that led to Wembley. The final against Crystal Palace produced an exciting 3-3 draw, before full back Lee Martin's strike decided the replay and secured Fergie's first trophy.

The Cup-Winners' Cup, European Super Cup and League Cup followed, yet the domestic title remained elusive until French striker Eric Cantona arrived from Leeds in November 1992. His nine goals in 24 starts contributed much to United's first title triumph for 26 years. That summer, Roy Keane came from Nottingham Forest to replace the Middlesbrough-bound Bryan Robson and partner Paul Ince in midfield. United stormed to a second Premier League title and thrashed Chelsea 4-0 in the FA Cup final to secure their first-ever Double.

A year later, Ferguson surprisingly allowed Hughes, Ince and Kanchelskis to leave after United lost the title to Blackburn and the FA Cup to Everton, although the failure was mainly caused by the absence of Cantona, banned for attacking a Crystal Palace fan in January.

Cantona made amends on his return, hitting seven goals in the last ten League matches to end Newcastle United's title challenge, and volleying the winner against Liverpool in the FA Cup final. Home-grown youngsters David Beckham, Paul Scholes and Gary Neville were also among the United players celebrating the second Double.

In 1996/97, United fell to Borussia Dortmund in the Champions League semi-finals but consoled themselves with another title, finishing seven points above Newcastle. When Cantona then quit football, aged just 31, £3.5 million Teddy Sheringham was drafted in from Tottenham. United built up a big lead in the Premiership and looked strong in Europe before injuries and fatigue ended their hopes in both.

Ferguson responded by investing over £23 million

Mark Hughes celebrates after scoring United's third in the 1990 FA Cup final against Palace

in Dutch centre-half Jaap Stam and Aston Villa striker
Dwight Yorke, whose devastating partnership with
Andy Cole yielded 53 goals. In a thrilling climax,
United clinched the title by beating Tottenham in
their last League match, the FA Cup with victory over
Newcastle and their first European Cup for over 30
years as injury time goals from super-subs Sheringham
and Ole Gunnar Solskjaer stunned Bayern Munich.
Ferguson was knighted after United's historic Treble.

The club's commercial activities were now in
overdrive. United had their own TV station. A £300
million kit deal with Nike cemented their position
as England's richest club. And Old Trafford would be
expanded to seat 76,000. In 1999/2000, United beat
Palmeiras to lift the Intercontinental Cup and strolled to
another title. But they were eliminated by Real Madrid
in the Champions League quarter-finals.

Their Premiership crown was retained in 2000/01
before Dutch striker Ruud van Nistelrooy and
Argentina playmaker Juan Sebastián Verón were snared
for a combined £47 million. Yet the surprise sale of
Stam to Lazio left the defence shaky. United failed to
beat Bayer Leverkusen in their European semi-final and
ended up empty-handed.

The next season, Van Nistelrooy's 44 goals in all
competitions spearheaded a successful title charge that
was also aided by the £33 million arrival of Leeds
centre half Rio Ferdinand. When Beckham was sold to
Real Madrid in the summer of 2003, Ferguson spent
half his £25 million fee on a rookie Portuguese winger,

Eric Cantona was the
catalyst for United's
long-awaited title
success

Cristiano Ronaldo, who headed the opener as United beat Millwall in the 2004 FA Cup Final. Another exciting young attacker, Wayne Rooney, arrived from Everton that summer, for £27 million.

In June 2005, the American sports tycoon Malcolm Glazer took over the club, plunging it deep into debt and causing resentment among many fans. On the field in 2005/06, United captured the League Cup as consolation for their failures elsewhere, while the good form of new goalkeeper Edwin van der Sar was another boon.

In the summer of 2006, £18 million midfielder Michael Carrick joined from Tottenham and proved an intelligent passer. As important was the emergence of Nemanja Vidic, signed from Spartak Moscow, as a dominant force alongside Ferdinand. But the season-defining contributions came from Ronaldo and Rooney, whose 23 goals apiece carried United to their first League title in four years.

The title defence was far from straightforward, despite the arrival of established internationals, midfielder Owen Hargreaves and striker Carlos Tévez, and bright young stars, midfielder Anderson and winger Nani, for a combined cost of over £60 million. Chelsea pulled level with two games left, but the Reds beat West Ham before clinching the title with a final-day success at Wigan. Ronaldo was outstanding, smashing an incredible 43 goals in all competitions, including the opener in the Champions League final against Chelsea in Moscow. A titanic struggle went

to extra time, then penalties, when Van der Sar was United's hero, saving from Nicolas Anelka to secure the club's third European Cup.

Seeking further success, Ferguson bought Bulgarian striker Dimitar Berbatov from Tottenham for £30.75 million. In December 2008, Rooney's precise finish saw off Liga de Quito in the final of the World Club Cup. Three months later United lifted the League Cup. The Champions League final had a less happy outcome, however. The Reds sorely missed the midfield energy of Darren Fletcher, wrongly red-carded in the semi-final defeat of Arsenal, as they were overrun by a majestic Barcelona in Rome.

Fergie and his team celebrate securing an unpredented treble at the 1999 Champions League final

After successive defeats in March, the Reds' Premier League title defence had also seemed in jeopardy. But a run of six straight wins, which included a stunning comeback from two goals down to Tottenham, got them back on track. A goalless home draw with Arsenal in the penultimate match sealed a hat-trick of Premiership crowns. The Reds had now equalled Liverpool's record of 18 titles.

However, United's chances of surpassing Liverpool and claiming an unprecedented fourth straight title were severely dented as Cristiano Ronaldo left for Real Madrid. His replacement, winger Luis Antonio Valencia (£16 million, from Wigan) did make a positive impact with his athleticism, commitment and ability to create chances, many of which were converted by the prolific Rooney, who plundered 34 goals in all competitions.

But the campaign unravelled during a miserable fortnight in late March and early April. First, United exited the Champions League at the quarter-finals to Bayern Munich, on away goals. Then, with Rooney injured, they lost to Chelsea and drew with Blackburn – effectively handing the title to the London club.

United had mounted a spirited fight in the face of severe injury problems and some debatable officiating in the clashes with Chelsea and Bayern – and retained the League Cup, memorably defeating City in the semi-final before overcoming Aston Villa at Wembley.

Equalling another north-west team's record of 18 league titles was particularly satisfying in 2009

Meanwhile, many fans were increasingly concerned that the club, which had previously enjoyed great financial security, was £716.5 million in debt under the ownership of the Glazer family. Protests were organised, with huge numbers of match-goers wearing the green and gold scarves of the anti-Glazer movement. As the season drew to a close the Red Knights, a consortium of affluent United-supporting business people, was reported to be putting the finishing touches to a £1.5 billion bid for the club.

GLORY GLORY MAN UTD

No club's fans can claim to be more witty and innovative when it comes to composing new songs and chants than those who follow United.

After Rafael Benítez's anti-Alex Ferguson rant during the 2008/09 campaign, United fans responded with: "He's crackin' up, He's crackin' up/He's crackin'/Rafa's crackin' up", to the tune of the Euro 96 hit *Football's Coming Home*. Liverpool's subsequent poor form helped United retain the title.

But many cherished songs are rooted in tradition. Past players like George Best and Eric Cantona are often celebrated. "We all live in a Georgie Best world" is chanted to the tune of The Beatles' *Yellow Submarine*. The many Cantona songs include a version of the *12 Days of Christmas* in which the true love has the sense to gift the appropriate number of Eric Cantonas each day.

Some players are immortalised in song despite modest Old Trafford careers, as is the case with Diego

Forlán. To the tune of *Volare*, "Di-e-go/oho/Di-e-go/oho/ He came from Uruguay/He made the Scousers cry" commemorates the striker's two goals in the Premier League victory at Anfield in December 2002. By contrast, Paul Ince is mocked for joining Liverpool a few years after his Old Trafford career ended. Whenever he faced United, the midfielder was reminded that he "used to play for a big club".

Club legends provide the inspiration for numerous songs

The ultimate composer of United songs is Pete Boyle, a diehard Red who tests out new songs and performs old favourites on match days at a pub called The Bishop Blaize, a stone's throw from Old Trafford. Such is Boyle's popularity that he has been booked to play full sets by supporters clubs in England, Ireland, Jersey and even Norway. "We sing about George Best, Willie Morgan, Paul Parker, David Beckham, Brian Kidd," Boyle said. "There are songs about Blackburn from 1994, about Newcastle from 1996. It's all about recording a club's history."

That history is important to fans keen to preserve the memories through the old songs. Matt Busby and the Busby Babes are still honoured often in songs like *United Calypso* ("Take a lesson, come and see/Football

Songs help to pass the club's history from generation to generation

taught by Matt Busby") and *Matt Busby's Aces*, sung to the tune of *Blaydon Races*. Like no other, this encapsulates the joy the Busby Babes gave. "All the lads and lasses/ With smiles upon their faces/Walking down the Warwick Road/To see Matt Busby's aces!" After delight turned to sadness, *Forever and Ever* mourned the Munich dead while keeping their memory alive. "In the cold snow of Munich/They laid down their lives/But they live on forever/In our hearts and our minds."

Manchester's tradition as a hotbed of musical talent is reflected in many United songs. "Giggs will tear you apart", to the tune of Joy Division's iconic *Love Will Tear Us Apart*, is an obvious favourite. Nor are United fans averse to a bit of cheesiness. Anderson is celebrated to the tune of Black Lace's nauseating 80s hit *Agadoo*. But instead of pushing pineapple and grinding coffee, they proclaim Anderson better than his compatriot Kleberson.

Several songs are regarded as official club anthems and have been recorded by the players to mark specific occasions. For instance, *Glory, Glory, Man United* – to the tune of *The Battle Hymn of the Republic*, with its famous refrain "Glory, Glory, Hallelujah" – was released before the 1983 FA Cup final. The single reached number 13 in the charts as United fans triumphantly bellowed out the chorus at Wembley.

The most caustic compositions are reserved for Liverpool (*In the Liverpool Slums*) and Manchester City (*This Is How It Feels To Be City*, to the tune of the Inspiral Carpets' *This Is How It Feels To Be Lonely*). As a former Liverpool player and manager of Manchester City and Newcastle, Kevin Keegan receives plenty of stick. *Cheer Up Kevin Keegan*, to the tune of The Monkees' *Daydream Believer*, was dreamt up after Keegan fumed that he would "love it" if Newcastle beat United in the 1995/96 title race. Towards the end of 2008/09, the song was adapted for Alan Shearer as he failed to save Newcastle from relegation.

By twice rejecting a move to United in his playing days, Shearer became the target of many chants. Most famously, Shearer's name is used in a song about Ole Gunnar Solskjaer, a striker who did join United in the summer of 1996. "You are my Solskjaer," fans still sing to the tune of *You Are My Sunshine.* "My Ole Solskjaer/ You make me happy/ When skies are grey/ Oh, Alan Shearer/ Was f***ing dearer/ Please don't take/My Solskjaer away." Like Solskjaer himself, the song is priceless.

Serenading the locals in front of Rome's Colosseum in 2009. Unfortunately, the team was not on song that night

HONOURS AND RECORDS

MAJOR HONOURS

WINNERS

Football League champions 1908, 1911, 1952, 1956, 1957, 1965, 1967

FA Premier League champions 1993, 1994, 1996, 1997, 1999, 2000, 2001, 2003, 2007, 2008, 2009

FA Cup 1909, 1948, 1963, 1977, 1983, 1985, 1990, 1994, 1996, 1999, 2004

Football League Cup 1992, 2006, 2009, 2010

European Champions Clubs' Cup 1968, 1999, 2008

European Cup-Winners' Cup 1991

European Super Cup 1991

World Club Cup 2008

Intercontinental Cup 1999

FA Charity/Community Shield 1908, 1911, 1952, 1956, 1957, 1983, 1993, 1994, 1996, 1997, 2003, 2008. Joint Holders 1965, 1967, 1977, 1990

Football League Division Two champions 1936, 1975

FA Youth Cup 1953, 1954, 1955, 1956, 1957, 1964, 1992, 1993, 2003

RECORDS

FOOTBALL LEAGUE RECORDS

- United share with Preston North End and Bristol City the record for the highest number of consecutive wins in the Football League – 14 in the old Second Division in 1904/05.
- **United lost 12 successive matches at the start of the 1930/31 Division One campaign. This remains a Football League record for defeats at the beginning of a season.**
- On 17th January 1948, 83,260 people crammed into Maine Road to see United draw 1-1 with Arsenal. This remains the highest attendance ever in the Football League.

PREMIER LEAGUE RECORDS

- United have won more Premier League titles than any other club, with 11. Next come Arsenal and Chelsea, with three.
- **The title has been won three times running on two occasions; 1999 -2001 and 2007-09 – a record.**
- United share the record for fewest home losses in a season – zero – with Arsenal and Chelsea. The Reds were unbeaten at Old Trafford in 1995/96 and 1999/2000.
- **In 1996/97, United's 77 points from 38 games was the lowest ever for Premier League title winners.**

- In 1994/95, United's 88 points from 42 games was the highest gained by a side not winning the title.
- **The record number of Premier League appearances for one club is held by Ryan Giggs. He played 544 times for United between the start of the Premiership in 1992 and 9 May, 2010.**
- Giggs is the premiership's most decorated player, with 11 winners' medals.
- **Giggs is the only player to have scored in every one of the Premiership's 18 seasons.**
- Giggs is one of three players to appear in every one of the Premiership's 18 seasons. The others are David James and Sol Campbell.
- **United conceded the first-ever Premier League goal on 15th August 1992, when Brian Deane scored for Sheffield United.**
- In 2007/08, Cristiano Ronaldo equalled Alan Shearer's Premier League record of 31 goals in a 38-game season.
- **On 4th March 1995, Andy Cole scored a record number of goals in a Premier League match, five against Ipswich Town. The record was later matched by Alan Shearer and Jermain Defoe.**
- That 9-0 thrashing of Ipswich is the biggest home win in the Premiership.
- **The record for most goals scored by a substitute was set by Ole Gunnar Solskjaer against Nottingham Forest on 6th February 1999. He scored four in the last ten minutes.**

- That 8-1 defeat of Forest is the biggest away win in Premier League history.
- **The record for goals in successive matches stands at ten, set by Ruud van Nistelrooy between March and August 2003.**
- In 2008/09, United set a record for the longest run without conceding a goal. Edwin van der Sar went 14 games and 1,311 minutes without letting in a goal.

CLUB RECORDS
- Record win: 10-0 against Anderlecht, 26th September, 1956, European Cup.
- **Record League win: 10-1 against Wolverhampton Wanderers, 15th October, 1892, First Division.**
- Record defeat: 7-0 to Blackburn Rovers, 10th April, 1926, First Division.

INDIVIDUAL RECORDS
- Most appearances (total): Ryan Giggs, 838 (1991-).
- **Most appearances (league): Bobby Charlton, 606 (1956-1973).**
- Most goals (total): Bobby Charlton, 249 (1956-1973).
- **Most goals (league): Bobby Charlton, 199 (1956-1973).**
- Most goals in a season (total): Denis Law, 46, 1963/64.
- **Most goals in a season (league): Dennis Viollet, 32, in 1959/60.**
- Oldest player: Billy Meredith, 46 years, 281 days, against Derby County, 7th May 1921.
- **Youngest goalscorer: Norman Whiteside, 17 years and seven days against Stoke City, 15th May 1982.**

- Most expensive signing: Dimitar Berbatov, from Tottenham Hotspur, £30.75million, 2008.
- **Record sale: Cristiano Ronaldo, to Real Madrid, £80 million, 2009.**
- European Footballer of the Year: Denis Law (1964), Bobby Charlton (1966), George Best (1968), Cristiano Ronaldo (2008).

ATTENDANCE RECORDS AT OLD TRAFFORD
- Old Trafford's attendance record was set on 25th March 1939 when 79,962 people saw the FA Cup semi-final between Wolves and Grimsby.
- **Old Trafford's capacity of 76,212 makes it the largest club ground in England.**
- United's defeat of Blackburn Rovers on 31st March 2007 was attended by 76,098 spectators, a Premier League record and Old Trafford's highest attendance as an all-seater.

OTHER ATTENDANCE RECORDS
- **On 17th January 1948, 83,260 people saw United draw 1-1 with Arsenal at Maine Road. This remains the highest ever attendance in the Football League.**

FA CUP RECORDS
- Biggest win: 8-0 against Yeovil Town, 12th February 1949.
- **Most appearances: Bobby Charlton, 78 (1956-73).**
- Most goals: Denis Law, 34 (1963-1973).
- **United have won the Cup 11 times – more than any other the club.**
- On 26th May 1983, Norman Whiteside became the youngest player to score in an FA Cup final, at 18 years and 18 days.

LEAGUE CUP RECORDS
- Biggest win: 7-2 against Newcastle United, 27th October 1976.

- **Most appearances: Bryan Robson, 51 (1981-1994).**
- Most goals: Brian McClair, 19 (1987-1997).
- **On 26th March 1983, Norman Whiteside became the youngest player to score in a League Cup final, at 17 years and 323 days.**

EUROPEAN RECORDS

- **Record win: 10-0 against Anderlecht, September 26, 1956, European Cup.**
- Most appearances (Champions League/European Cup): Ryan Giggs (left), 125 (1993-).
- **Most goals (all competitions): Ruud van Nistelrooy, 38 (2000-2005).**
- Most goals (Champions League/European Cup): Ruud van Nistelrooy, 38 (2000-2005).

FIRSTS

- On 12th September 1956, United became the first English club to enter European competition, winning 2-0 at Anderlecht in the European Cup.
- **On 29th May 1968, United became the first English club to lift the European Cup, beating Benfica 4-1.**
- On 26th May 1999, United became the first English club to complete the Treble, as they beat Bayern Munich 2-1 in the European Cup final.
- Dennis Viollet's hat-trick in the 10-0 victory over Anderlecht on 26th September 1956 was the first to be scored in European competition by an Englishman.
- On 18th May 1985, Kevin Moran was the first player to be sent off in an FA Cup final, for tripping Everton's Peter Reid.
- **On 21st May 1977, Martin Buchan became the first player to captain Cup-winning sides north and south of the border in the post-war period. Having won the Scottish Cup with Aberdeen, Buchan skippered United as they defeated Liverpool 2-1.**
- Bryan Robson was the first player in the 20th century to captain three FA Cup-winning sides, in 1983, 1985 and 1990.
- **The 1993 Premier League triumph meant Alex Ferguson was the first manager to win League titles north and south of the border.**
- In May 1996, United became the first team to win the League and Cup Double twice.
- **On 30th November 1999, United beat Palmeiras of Brazil 1-0 to become the first British winners of the Intercontinental Cup.**
- Ruud van Nistelrooy was the first player to score in eight consecutive Premiership matches, between 12th December 2001 and 19th January 2002.
- **On 21st December 2008, a 1-0 defeat of Liga de Quito of Ecuador meant United were the first English winners of the World Club Cup.**